# Essays
## on
# Nature and Grace

# Essays
# on
# Nature and Grace

by

Joseph Sittler

FORTRESS PRESS

Philadelphia

*Library of Congress Catalog Card Number 76–171505*

*ISBN 0–8006–0070–3*

3273C72     Printed in the United States of America     1-70

**TO JEANNE**

# Table of Contents

# Introduction

This book is an effort to relate the ancient doctrine of the grace of God to the experience of man in the world of nature. The classical formulations of that doctrine were made long before man's understanding of nature and his manipulation of its elements and forces achieved the crucial role in his life that they presently have. What centuries of Christian reflection have felt and thought about God's grace is not to be repudiated. But the doctrine must be relocated for our time, and a fresh way must be found to propose the reality of grace to men who understand the cosmos as a closed system.

The old theological rubric of "Nature and Grace" did not have to attend to Copernicus, Newton, Darwin, Marx, Freud, or to the world- and self-understanding which has been engendered by the knowledge and insight these names represent. As late as Luther and Calvin, that rubric could still put the problem and deal with it according to the fundamental terms of the catholic centuries. The question Luther and Calvin asked was not different from that raised by their fathers all the way from St. Paul to St. Thomas Aquinas. The natural-world matrix of the issue was the same, and they asked: How does the disposition and power of a gracious God impact upon, penetrate, change, and redeem sinful man?

Man is a sinner, and he lives in a world. But his life in that world has become literally a new kind of life. Where is grace in this world that has been experimentally taken apart by empirical science, its laws disclosed, its structure and process translated into statistical terms, and the knowledge of which, even if fragmentary, is sufficient to secure predictability and enable fantastically complicated manipulation of its forces and processes? Is it possible to reconceptualize, expand, experience, and bear witness to the grace of God within a world that is beheld and practically dealt with as a closed system? That is the issue to which these chapters are addressed.

The ecological issue is introduced, not because that issue solves the problem, but because it forces the problem upon the mind's attention. Reflection upon grace does not depend upon viewing the world as an ecosystem; the world as an ecosystem provides the fateful occasion for such fresh reflection. When, therefore, in the pages to follow, the ecological facts of life are alluded to, such allusions are not introduced as arguments for the reality of grace; they are rather descriptions of the *field* of grace, expositions of the actuality of man's life and placement within the web of nature. The life of man so placed, related, and embedded constitutes a factual precondition to the kind of speech about grace which has the possibility really to address him.

The title, *Essays on Nature and Grace,* is a way of saying to the reader something about procedure and style. The word "essays" announces that no single starting point is fixed, that a variety of perspectives are employed, that whatever force the argument has is cumulative and symbiotic. Style of presentation, while a kind of obedience to differences in data, is more than that. For what is necessary is to reenact in representation in language the order or disorder, the logic or accidental sequence by which facts, events, and relations invite new reflections on previously solidified themes.

Alfred North Whitehead once remarked that ". . . style is the morality of the mind." He was saying that style is not a formal addition to the operation of sensibility and mind but is of the very substance and lively nature of their working in a man. If, in the pages to follow, there is a certain looseness, a seeming leap from one kind of data to another, an unusual putting together of facts and reflections that seem on the surface to be far apart, a symbiosis of insights that are biblical, historical, poetical, practical—in short, if the style of these chapters seems out of step with prevailing mores in theological exposition, I can only say that these peculiarities are a way of being "moral." For in writing about a theme in a way that shall reenact in diction and vocabulary the living process by which that theme emerged, unfolded, intersected, became enforced and modified by others, one owes to honesty the effort to expound what comes out of his mind in a style appropriate to the fundamental unsystematic of the way it entered his mind. The matter, that is to say, not only controls the manner; it is dependent upon it for right release.

The perils of this stylistic path are clearly known to me; I live my life among articulate colleagues and students who forcibly remind me of them. I choose to disobey with my eyes open. A model professor professes and practices his competence around a well-defined item within an enormous web. He is most clear about the item if he ignores the web! But to have a mind that honors that way of working and at the same time retains a sense of humor about that way's adequacy to the kind of Christian theme he wants to express and about the receiving equipment of the community to which the address is made, is to be forced to open up theological speech according to the requirements of the theme itself.

The "web" apart from which I cannot think, or think about thinking, is the ecological structure of the human reality. The term "ecology" has a transphysical meaning. It points with undismissable stubbornness to the *context* of all things; it insists that no thing exists apart from all things. All orders have uncertain edges, all categories leak, all propositions conceal a presupposition, or an aware or unaware limitation within which alone they are accurate or represent truth.

The recognition that one is in deepest nature vehemently ecological is a recognition that cannot without betrayal be distorted by style or denied. It is to that danger that Whitehead points in his aphorism that "... style is the morality of the mind." Something of the same ecological embeddedness of thought informs George Santayana's statement in the introduction to a little volume of his work. He was speaking of the formal conventionality of his poems, and explained, "If their prosody is warm and traditional, like a liturgy, it is because they represent the initiation of a mind into a world older and larger than itself; not the chance experiences of an individual, but his submission to what is not his chance experience, to the truth of nature, and to the moral heritage of mankind."[1] Santayana's poems, that is to say, are not episodic expostulations; they are "like a liturgy"—having a language and a quiet rhythm that honors the life and experience of men long dead and the immemorial continuities that persist through change.

About a hundred years ago William James, in a Harvard College lecture, declared that:

> The real world as it is given objectively at this moment is the sum total of all its being and events now. But can we think of such a sum? Can we realize for an instant what a cross-section of all existence at a definite point of time would be? While I talk and the flies buzz, a sea gull catches a fish at the mouth of the Amazon, a tree falls in the Adirondack wilderness, a man sneezes in Germany, a horse dies in Tartary, and twins are born in France. What does that mean? Does the contemporaneity of these events with one another, and with a million others as disjointed, form a rational bond between them, and unite them into anything that means for us a world? Yet just such a collateral contemporaneity, and nothing else, is the real order of the world. It is an order with which we have nothing to do but to get away from it as fast as possible. As I said, we break it: we break it into histories, and we break it into arts, and we break it into sciences; and then we begin to feel at home.[2]

All my life I have sought a form of theological discourse which should be obedient in style to James's *dictum,* especially "collateral contemporaneity." And when one seeks, as I presently do, to articulate the immediacy of grace, to interiorize the objective reality of the dogma so that it shall become forceful for our time's need to stand *within* the creation as we receive redemption, the difficulty becomes enormous. For theological exposition itself is ordered, sequential discourse, but the gifts of grace whereby grace is apprehended, acknowledged, and allowed to focus sensibility and excite reflection—these are not ordered or sequential. The life-liveliness of a thing-becoming is not the same as the static status of a thing-become. And a way must be found to reenact in the style of the report the wild unsystematic of the occurrence.

One must, to be sure, seek order. The election of a discursive rather than a logical sequence does not deny this necessity. But the order imposed must be appropriate to the end sought. The reality of disorder in the "collateral contemporaneity" must not be repudiated or forgotten. It is this effort to make the style of utterance appropriate to contemporary sensibility that characterizes the "disordered-order" one finds in modern poetry, the short story, the novel, current nonconsecutive humor, and drama. Language has to be sprung open to the fact, the chaos, the novelty of experience. The serene diction of Jane Austen would not serve to represent in language the life-pace and shocks of our time. All uses of language are an imposition of order. And all language comes short of what it would communicate. In even its most ample and precise exercise language is a verbal groping for sufficiency, a grammar stalking elusive relations, flung loops of sentences tightening around the undulant and the evanescent.

I should like, then, to set down the bundle of components that have determined a central theme. It is sometimes the case that one's reflections upon problems, crises, and experiences are troubled by a persistent suspicion that they are all related, that facts and relations lack definition and move so slowly toward conceptual resolution because the reality in which they have their unity has not declared itself.

In virtue of what gift, love, understanding, and appropriate behavior can man live with the world-as-nature so as rightly to enjoy and use it? That is the problem. It is the thesis of these chapters that nothing short of a radical relocation and reconceptualization of the reality and the doctrine of grace is an adequate answer to that problem. The following chapter is a recounting of the components, separately and in interaction, which have entered into the solidification of that conviction.

The invitation by the Harvard University Committee for the William Belden Noble Lectureship to deliver a series of lectures in 1958 was the occasion for my first effort to draw together some questions about the communicability of the doctrine of God's grace in a world so radically different from the world within which the doctrine was first shaped. Not much of the substance of those lectures has survived the intervening years. But the courtesy of that invitation is remembered with gratitude, and the stimulus the occasion afforded is here acknowledged.

The opportunity, in 1964, to deliver the Gray Lectures at the Divinity School of Duke University, was the occasion to investigate the relation between grace and ethics, and in the lectures there I attempted to suggest what in the discussion that follows is more explicitly worked out.

# 1.

# The Emergence of a Theme

During the years 1951–1966 I was a member of the Faith and Order Commission of the World Council of Churches. Because the first and most public of the components that have forced me to reexamine the doctrine of grace became clear in the Faith and Order Assemblies, I shall begin with a report of that experience.

## Faith and Order: Christology in Motion

The Faith and Order Movement, inaugurated at Lausanne in 1927, devoted its first decade-and-a-half to a series of studies on the *Nature of the Church*. The maturation of these studies had, by 1950, made completely clear that the church is a christological reality. That acknowledgment resulted in the establishment in Europe, Asia, and North America of new study groups directed to inquire into the now restated theme, *Christ and the Church*. But these groups, too, after almost a decade of investigation of the biblical, church-historical, and dogmatic foundations of Christology, found that their task resisted solution within even the broad terms of the expanded title. The meaning, role, intention, presence, and biblically attested *scope* of the christological reality demanded an even larger setting and reference. *Christ and the Church,* that is to say, was disclosed as an insufficient rubric under which to deal with the themes and energies which the church itself knows and celebrates.

In the grip of that realization, and under appointment to prepare an address for the Assembly of the World Council of

Churches at <u>New Delhi, India in 1961,</u> I made an initial effort to relate christological ascriptions of praise and power to the reality of man's existence within the world-as-nature and the world-as-history.[1] That address, not representative of any then articulated strand of ecumenical thought, proposed the thesis that only a Christology capable of administering the cosmic scope of biblical and catholic Christ-testimony would be adequate to the question about Christ and his meaning as it is necessarily put by men of modernity.

For among the many things one means by "modern," a capital reality is this: that man's transactions with the natural world are so vast, penetrating, and revolutionary in his actuality as person, worker, thinker, and world-manipulator that it is required of any religious interpretation of life and world that it intersect with and attend to these changes. Several sentences from that address suggest the central thrust.

> . . . The way forward is from Christology expanded to its cosmic dimensions, made passionate by the pathos of this threatened earth, and made ethical by the love and the wrath of God. For as it was said in the beginning that God beheld all things and declared them good, so it was uttered by an angel of the Apocalypse of St. John, ". . . ascending from the east, having the seal of the living God: and he cried with a loud voice to whom it was given to hurt the earth and the sea, saying, hurt not the earth, neither the sea, nor the trees. . . ." The care of the earth, the realm of nature as a theater of grace, the ordering of the thick, material procedures that make available to or deprive men of bread and peace—these are Christological obediences before they are practical necessities.[2]

During the two years that intervened between the World Council of Churches Assembly at New Delhi and the meeting of the Faith and Order Commission at Montreal in 1963, the call for a doctrine of grace appropriate to modern man's operational reality with the world-as-nature excited a considerable body of discussion. Biblical scholars were both supportive and critical: some said that the interpretation of the New Testament witness to the scope and operation of God's grace was restricted to the realm of redemption; others felt that the realm of creation was also a legitimate theatre for an encounter with grace.[3]

At Montreal in 1963 a very vigorous biblical and theological debate, while not advancing the issue toward solution, guaranteed that the confinement of the meaning of the grace of God within the category *Christ and the Church* was no longer useful. In an address to a Faith and Order meeting in Aarhus, Denmark in 1964, the Commission's Secretary, Dr. Lukas Vischer said that while ". . . of course we agree that the revelation in Christ is the center of our faith, the course and the life of the church . . . how are we to think of the relationship between God's creating and redeeming activity? What do we mean when we call Christ the Lord of the whole world?"[4]

One of the section reports of the Aarhus Assembly signalized the inevitability of a cosmic-context as alone sufficient for an examination of the scope of grace when it proposed for future Faith and Order study the theme, *Creation, New Creation, and the Unity of the Church.* The report that supported the proposal reads, in part, as follows:

> Man's selfhood has always been deeply informed by his common transactions with the world-as-nature: extracting, cultivating, fabricating, producing, consuming, and, above all, forever wondering about the structure and processes of this environment of his historical existence.
>
> In our times these transactions have achieved such penetration and manipulative efficiency that their exercise is as heavy with peril as it is astounding in promise. From subatomic investigations on to galactic speculations, from the infinitely small to the incredibly large—these are the brackets within which the term *nature* has its present meaning.
>
> This enormous expansion of the phenomenology of the world-as-nature confronts Christian theology with a clamant task: she must expound the doctrines of creation and new creation with a bigness and subtlety appropriate to the enhanced range of modern man's mental life.

Scientific thought operates with models which are ultimately unverifiable; there is no necessary connection between the thoughts in the mind and the way things are. But the ordinary man does not know this; and the empirical and amazing results of scientific work stand before him with operational clarity. Powers of nature have been open as never before to be used and conquered by man's will. The life of nature has more and more been drawn into the life of history. This new relationship of man to nature has incalculable consequences for good; on the other hand, especially in the corporate and institutional ways of man's dealing with the world, there is a corresponding, and terrifying, increase in the potentialities of evil.[5]

The preceding citation demonstrates clearly the shift, movement, and direction out of which the chapters to follow were born. Christology is here set in a ring of vastly enlarged scope; the doctrine of creation is proposed as the *only* adequate referential context for Christology; world-change, new tasks and new hopes, are acknowledged under the term "new creation." The "unity of the church"—that ancient dream—is now envisioned and sought, not along a path that travels only inward and along the way of the church's past, but rather along the path upon which man is now moving, rich with astounding scientific and social knowledge, and complicated by novel contexts for world decision.

## Christology and Creation

The incitements to christological reflection which have occurred by participation in the ecumenical scene illustrate but do not by any means exhaust the components that must be noted.

Long before I began to work as a teacher of Christian theology I had the obligation as a parish pastor regularly to preach on the appointed pericopes for the church year. During those years I became fascinated with the rhetorical fullness of the testimony to Christ, the variety of conceptualizations in which it is set forth by and for the mind of the community, the alluring richness with which the fullness of Christ was celebrated. I felt then, and have

not been able to overcome the certainty, ~~that no dogmatical order-~~
~~ing is even faintly adequate to the multiple facets of that testimo~~ny.

During my years as a teacher the conviction has been growing
and gaining substance that the almost exclusive elaboration of
Christology under the article of redemption is reductive of biblical
scope and of the richness of theological tradition. Such exclusive-
ness is not calculated to propose to the contemporary mind and
interest the salvatory scope, meaning, and power of Christ. An
elaboration of that conviction is the content of this entire study;
but some indication of the variety of perspective from which it has
emerged and been formed ought in a preliminary way be undertaken.

Particularly troubling, and particularly ignored, diminished, or
displaced in the interest of controlling dogmatic traditions in the
West, are the following: the image of faith's life as life in the
body, *en christo*; the testimony in Ephesians, Colossians, and elsewhere which suggests that the pattern of creation-redemption-
sanctification is constrictive of the organismic biblical speech
about the presence and power of the grace of God in Christ; the
language of the Fourth Gospel, particularly when read contrapun-
tally with the testimony of the Epistles. When an effort is made
to locate the roots and resonances of that language in the community of Israel that stands behind it, and in the religious desire
for ontological clarity and cosmical amplitude that was clamant
in the world around it, one finds it possible and legitimate to see
a growing magnitude in the christological utterances of the New
Testament. This coherence and growth is structured by an ever-
widening orbit of christological meaning, scope, and force. From
the interpretation that asserts that in Christ, God ". . . has helped
his servant, Israel, in remembrance of his mercy . . ." (Luke 2:54)
there grows an enormously expanded language of claim and
rhetoric of praise that does not stop short of ". . . his purpose
which he set forth in Christ as a place for the fullness of time,
to unite all things in him, things in heaven and things on earth"
(Eph. 1:10).

## The Christology of the Eastern Church

It is, I think, correct to assert that for most of Western Christendom the Fathers are read in relation to, and their thought assumed under, the conceptions solidified at Chalcedon. Specialists know that, and they regularly instruct us about the rich variety in the patristic literature and of the radically different mode of thought that characterized the Eastern Fathers. But until one's curiosity is furnished by experience of the piety, liturgy, and strangely social christological language of Orthodox thought and devotion, he is not forced deeper than the level of those generalizations about patristic theology that ordinarily constitute instruction in theological schools.[6]

When, however, such a disturbance has taken place, and when one attends to the Eastern Fathers themselves, he moves into a fresh world of discourse. Christological reflection is among them elaborated in such a way as to draw into a unity certain basic notions of St. Paul. The *body*, life in the body by participation, the spirit as the modality of the *Presence, reenactment* as a model for the Christian life—these notions and images are intrinsically incapable of realization within Western "means" of grace, or any rigid *ordo salutis*.

This indubitably apostolic strand of christological reflection—unknown, or neglected, or suppressed in the development of dogma in the West—is not mentioned here because of any bizarre notion that I have the competence to add anything to what my betters have done and are doing! It is mentioned because in ecumenical assemblies, in many long sessions with theologians of the churches of the East, in frequent participation in Orthodox liturgy, and in subsequent reflection, I have been forced to ask what kind of proposition might articulate the actuality of the grace of the indwelling Christ in the common events of nature, history, and society as adoration of this grace is celebrated in those opulent and nuanced liturgical forms.

The sheer vitality and luminousness of the Christology of the East has been not only a powerful motivation to inquiry into the work of Nyssa, Irenaeus, Cyril, and other Eastern Fathers, but also formative of the conviction that within this Eastern tradition is a language of christological witness that intersects precisely with questions that press upon the church's thought today. In a later chapter this conviction will be more fully detailed.

## The Doctrine of Grace

Theology has spoken of grace in steady correlation with such manifestations of human need as have given interior sense to the term. For instance: Grace is the empowerment of salvation by God, and its working is unfolded in structures parallel to man's knowledge of damnation. Grace is God's seeking and finding man as the lost one. Grace is God's benevolent disposition toward and action on behalf of man who is trapped in evil; grace is the forgiveness of sins. Grace is the surety of God's reality and meaning when damnation takes the form of meaninglessness. Grace is the placement of man in a community of redemption and reconciliation when abandonment and isolation is the form of the human hurt. Grace is the supply of strength when weakness is characteristic of the human effort. Grace is the *yes* of the evangel to every *no* of the world-within, the world-among, and the impenetrable world-around. Grace is the presence of the eternal in the evanescence of the temporal. Grace is the promise and power of life at the moment of death—even of those little dyings that occur before death. Grace is intrinsic in all that God has made. When encountered in his deed of grace in Jesus Christ, it so places the child of grace within existence that the world of persons, things, processes, and all mortal engagements with them is proposed to the mind and spirit as a veritable theatre of grace.

Every sentence in that paragraph enfolds a large testimony of the church's long reflection upon and experience of grace. Every sentence points, also, toward past traditions that are presently waning, to terms whose onetime precision has become vague, to experiences that no longer find the word "grace" generally intelligible to a world-picture, and a practical operational life so within its powerful grip, that the very idea of grace is strange. The late Professor Joseph Haroutunian described this strangeness as follows:

> The traditional paradox of grace and freedom has become academic. When a man sets out to achieve a given good, he looks for the suitable means to do it, and "grace," the favor and agency of God, is not one of them. What a man needs is a certain combination of knowledge, skill, opportunity, power, and the freedom to make use of them. No man will trust his good to grace, and no man will question his freedom provided he has ability and is not prevented from using it.
>
> When we are able to do what we will, we know ourselves as free, and when we are free, we need no grace. When we are unable to achieve our ends, we do not turn to a supernatural power but try to devise some new means that will give us success. Failure is a call, not to prayer, but to renewed calculation and effort. If success appears beyond our reach, we prefer to "accept the facts" rather than resort to "faith," which savors of superstition. If a miracle were to give us the success we seek, we should be greatly surprised or even discomfited. Hence, grace as supernatural or divine power is not what we live by, and freedom, the opportunity to act, has nothing to do with it.[7]

That mordant but accurate statement strongly suggests that the plentitude of the reality of grace and the broad theatre of its engagement with thought and sensibility has not commonly been declared with a scope appropriate either to the magnitude of the energy of grace or in sufficiently precise relation to the changes in contemporary man's self-understanding. For that self-understanding has been traumatized by modern man's aggressive and fateful transactions with the world-as-nature. Rather, indeed, the doctrine of grace has been almost exclusively administered in relation to man as sinner. So to declare the reality of grace is by no means an error. If there is no grace of God for radical evil no other or ampler presentation of it can be effectual for fundamental human fact. But if grace is suggested as exhausting its meaning and redemptive force at that point alone, entire ranges of it remain unadministered.

The reality of grace is proposed intelligibly to a generation only when the terms of the proposal are correlative—even if negatively, judgmentally, or diagnostically—to the actuality of man in his subjective acknowledgment of how he is and stands and feels and works and thinks and acts in the world. It is a concern of these essays so to describe the actuality of man in his existence in an aggressive and open stance amidst, and even managerially above, the world of nature, as to prescind what unadministered dimensions of grace must again be proclaimed if the word of the grace of God is to be intelligible or even interesting.

These statements about grace anticipate and require what must be examined in a study of nature. At this preliminary point it will suffice only to propose that if grace is to be an intelligible word of redemption, and if the human person to whom that word is addressed defines and knows himself in ever more profound, precise, and fateful transactions with the world-as-nature, then the place of operation of his existence cannot be excluded from whatever redemption is to be meaningful. Man in orbit among the stars, and man in fascinated probing among the complexities of the genetic code is a creature who, to be sure, is no fraction less an alienated and egocentric sinner than his fathers have been! But science utilized forward into an even more elaborate technology presents us with a creature for whom a spatial transcendentality is not persuasive. For such a man traditional eschatology is unrelated to vital concerns. Moral judgment and counsel require clear and challenging relation to responsibilities stated in terms of unparalleled powers, anxieties, terrors, and possibilities. The theological *grammar of grace* is reportorial of redemption; the language and *rhetoric of grace* must be made congruent to the

potentiality and operational actuality of man in his contemporary
placement amidst his own artifactual world of operations.

Considerations such as the foregoing also imply several questions about the adequacy of the categories of traditional Christian
ethics. Systems of Christian ethics have most generally been
elaborated out of a natural law postulate coordinated with a
doctrine of the divine creation, or out of a more biblically oriented
sin-grace pattern in which the Incarnation is the appearing, the
mandate, the model, and the power whereby the righteousness
of God is given to man and required of him. Both patterns have
been able by means of principles, models, and existential analysis
of the decisive "ought" as clarified by situationally focused
demands, to speak to man of the righteousness of God and to
call and direct him to obedience to it.

But both of these large ways in ethics have become less and less
commanding and clear, not because they are wrong theologically,
but because they are anachronistic anthropologically. What God
requires of man does not change. But the context of life with the
fellowman, the institutionalization of effective structures of relationships whereby effectiveness of actual obedience to the will
of God can be realized—these have changed. What God wills is
movingly symbolized by the cup of cold water, but what that will
requires in content and practical procedure is no longer clear
under that symbol.

It is here argued that ethical clarity is a function of descriptive
accuracy. One cannot see the dimensions of what he ought if he is
deluded about the dimensions of what he is. And while it would
be ungrateful and irresponsible to affirm that our fathers in
ethical counsel have not spoken to man's reality, it would be
equally irresponsible to assume that contemporary man's reality
can be specified apart from the social and psychological facts in
the grip of which his self-awareness, and with it his problem, is
made actual. Some decades of reflection have made it quite clear
that man is who he is and what he is, not only in virtue of some

essence, structure, or relation specified in terms only of his God-relationship, but that he is what he is because he exists *where* he is. He lives in a nexus of human relations and nature relations in which sheer operational facticity pierces into and deeply complicates all efforts to discern, clarify, and respond to the righteousness of God.

If recent enrichments have accrued to older ontological notions in virtue of contemporary man's assessment that his being-in-the-world is a "horizon" of his reality, then this being-in-the-world must be given blunt empirical substance and rescued from abstraction by the facts. The primary fact is that "in" the world is not a sufficient statement to announce *how* contemporary man is "in" the world. He is in the world as a creature who, for the first time, has the structures and powers of the natural world sufficiently and growingly within his manipulative grasp to form it toward an order for human life of dreamlike potentialities, or to utilize his knowledge-power toward an unimaginable hell.

Is there within the fullness of the biblical witnesses to the reality and work of grace the possibility to reinterpret the doctrine forward into contemporary knowledge and experience? Can the doctrine be enfolded in terms, and so explicated within self- and world-understanding as to escape the no longer expressive categories that characterize traditional notions: created and uncreated grace, infused and forensic grace, grace as private-individual gift, and "common grace"? Might it be possible, along with such reinterpretation, to recover and release such an understanding and celebration of grace as shall locate its presence and power and hope within man's life in the world-as-creation as well as within man's hearing and receiving of grace through the Word and sacrament of forgiveness?

Such a possibility not only exists; the dynamics of it are folded deeply within the heart of the biblical witness and have been attested by presently muted voices in the history of Christian reflection. In the appropriate place this assertion will be so placed

into continuity with biblical and patristic evidences as to support
the assertion and defend it from the charge of innovation.

Men are not saved by an ever-so-excruciating awareness that
they are lost. The knowledge of damnation does not of itself
generate the powers of redemption. But such knowledge may
supply the conceptual tools and suggest the linguistic modes for
effective proposal of the reality of grace. When, for instance, a
young man in one of my classes, attending a lecture on "Grace
and Incarnation," expostulated, "If it were true it would do," he
placed himself, perhaps unwittingly, exactly at the point to which
theology aspires. For all self-clarifying speech intersecting with
grace-clarifying witnesses is the perennial and ever-changing
theological "moment."

Knowledge gained by man's probing into the structure and
process of the physical world, the accumulation of evolutionary,
genetic, psychological, and social facts is so astounding as to
shatter the sufficiency of older ways of specifying and relating
grace and nature and, on the positive side, suggests a quite fresh
and more comprehensive anthropology. While it may not be
possible for our generation to fashion for its day and necessity a
systematic and an ethics that shall have the coherent authority
of older systems, it may be possible by working obediently to
wait creatively. In biblical understanding, to wait does not
guarantee the arrival of what one waits for, but it is not thereby
negative or static. Waiting and hoping belong together (in Hebrew
the same root word) ; to wait is a stance that works and hopes and
remembers promises. As a specific agenda for the theologian such
a constructive waiting is not a stasis; it is a clear task to be done:
to state the problem in actual terms and in right dimensions and
proportions.

## The "Unaccredited" Witness

The strange title for this section is simply a blunt way of saying
that the admittance of literary modes of seeking and speaking

truth to the company of those who engage in grave theological discourse is, by many theologians, viewed with something short of enthusiasm. This chapter has the task of naming the components that have entered into the resolution to write a book, and it is neither possible nor honest to disguise what the inquiry owes to those who, in the practice of literary art, have been tutorial to what insights may appear.

But something more must be said if one is to avoid too low and too incidental an evaluation of what I think to be actual operations of grace as these work within that anguished and joyous act of recognition of truth to which serious literature aspires.

As theologian and as preacher, literature has never been for me merely a mine of felicitous articulation of things that have been elsewhere learned; it has itself been a place of listening and learning. That throughout one's life he should have been sensitive to grace in the speech of men because in another, a prior, and a more splendid place he had already been found by grace and attuned to its motions may be joyfully acknowledged as but the working-out of the prevenience and the invenience of the grace of God. But that acknowledgment must not diminish the debt one owes to, or modify the integrity and particularity of, the literary act. Grace is always a strangeness, a gift, a surprise. Because literature is life and truth "drawn heavy and dripping from the waters of sentiency," *its* mode of recognition, so different from theological discourse, dramatizes that strangeness, makes that gift the more astounding and that surprise the more sudden. That statement is simply true; and the call of liturgy, hymnody, chant, and the centuries-long effort to blend the sonority of transoccasional speech with the substance of occasion-born petition in the prayers of the church is a sufficient proof of it. I shall not, in a later section, argue the general point that the presence of grace is beheld and celebrated in and through the creation, and is specifically named as a grace. I shall, rather, adduce the direct evidence of literary art.

## "Theological Method"

The quotation marks are added because in these latter days some declaration on the subject is desired, even demanded, and the demand gains in vehemence according to the youth of the student. My own disinclination to state a theological method is grounded in the strong conviction that one does not devise a method and then dig into the data; one lives with the data, lets their force, variety, and authenticity generate a sense for what Jean Daniélou calls a "way of knowing" appropriate to the nature of the data. An enduring memory is an evening spent with a group of graduate students who had invited Professor Paul Tillich, then in his seventy-third year, for a round of discussion. To the aggressive demand of several students that he state forthwith his theological method, Professor Tillich replied that the student was asking that something be supplied at the beginning of the sentence that could only come at the end! He added that he himself had not even raised the methodological question until he was two-thirds of the way toward the completion of his *Systematic Theology*!

Every theologian, to be sure, has a theological method, but the clarity and permeative force of it is likely to be disclosed even to himself only in the course of his most mature work. When that method does become clear it will be seen to have been a *function of a disposition toward the evaluation of data* in their living historical force, and not an imposition of abstract norms for "truth" or "authenticity" arrived at early and exercised consistently.

This "disposition toward the evaluation of data" is a profound, largely subterranean thing. To the elements that enter into its formation we cannot here long attend, but some allusion to them will perhaps suffice to complicate into becoming modesty any who suppose that "theological method" is a coolly chosen procedure elected to regnancy in a kind of "hard gem-like flame" of pure reason. The dynamics of a disposition, if traced to their roots (and this effort of itself discloses matters long forgotten or suppressed that lie at least "full fathom five"), are formed in large part by the majesty and gravity, or the banality and superficiality, of one's earliest memory of the Christian story in private and public encounters with it. Who can exactly measure the extent to which interplay between historical, humanistic, experiential authenticity and specifically Christian episodes, symbols, and dogmas served to open and lure the mind or to constrict and offend it? Mature intellectual angers are often the persisting resonance of adolescent violations or distortions. Later clarity about these may be unable to disengage such occasions from the negative feeling-tone from which, even when disclosed, one is unable to free himself.

When certain theologians speak of a *Vorverständnis* one is not certain of the compass of forces they mean to enclose. I am quite certain, however, that I should enclose in the term as very important, elements which are protected from public view by such a sonorous term as *Vorverständnis* and thus hidden and inoperative as help between writer and reader. This is only to say that every man has a dispositional bent which, when acknowledged, goes a long way toward understanding what one historian has called "the mystery of the mind's attention." Why does one person "attend" to what another does not? Is there an interior, quite inaccessible, calculus of sensitivity which accounts for this difference? Is the difference not a product of the persistence of some facts of experience and the waning of others, the instant and commanding authority of a particular pattern of words so that one constellation of data is roused from sleep by its occurring and resonates back to it, while equally well-attested data of experience remain in the dormitory of memory?

If, then, thus self-warned I were to say anything further about the theological method which informs these essays, I should have to acknowledge that I do not have one that deserves accreditation by the voting members of the reigning methodological club. "Methodology" understood as a starting point that is fixed, explication of all things from the chosen starting point that remains unembarrassed by historical change, systematic rigidity that is more congruent with structures of nature than with the realities of history—from all that I flee as fast as possible!

Regardless, however, of one's impatience with the methodological clamor, one does have a way of putting things together. He is aware that his work, satisfying to himself or not—and commonly not—discloses a kind of order. Is it possible to say what this is and how it works?

Theology is the proposal of relations between the testimony of a community of faith and the life of man in nature and in history. The clarification and authentication of both substantives—the testimony of the community and the life of man—will take place, if it does take place, in the process and according to the amplitude and depth of the congruities disclosed in those relations as actually unfolded. One does, indeed, have a starting point chronologically; but the establishment and securing of the legitimacy of that starting point accrues to it as a function of the relations deployed in following out its suggestions. The pattern is more like a symbiosis than an equation or a graph. Theology is the proposal of a symbol-counterpoint; it secures persuasiveness by two achievements: the clarification of an interior coherence among those symbols that open the depth of the testimony of faith, and by the antiphonal voices of recognition it arouses. Substantives are not nakedly proposed; terms gather substance by the amplification of their reality-as-relations. If this is not the nature of affirmation about God, man, grace, redemption, and other major *loci,* then I have radically misread both Bible and Christian fact.

# 2.

# Grace in the Scriptures

When one sets out to describe the meanings and energies designated by the term "grace" he confronts a simple but powerful impediment. Most Christians first heard the word in preaching or in catechism or some other adolescent or earlier situation. And when the Old Testament is directly read we commonly come at it via the New Testament. What is said in the Gospels and Epistles about the grace of God so fills the term that pre-New Testament statements about God and his grace are either not attended to (because the term "grace" is not an Old Testament term) or are subsumed under the grace-Christ rubric so firmly as to invite the mind to suppose that before Christ, and without Christ, grace does not exist.

This "location" of the term continues to operate reductively at more sophisticated levels. Trinitarian formulations have begot a triadic sequence of creation, redemption, sanctification. Appropriate and useful as this triad may be for Christian theology, the application of it to the experience of Israel—and the more unconscious the more obscuring—pulls into wrong proportions the Old Testament way of understanding God, the power and scope of the goodness of God, and the implications of faith in him for the formal ethics of Israel and for her mode of life in its various cultic manifestations. In the Old Testament the magnetic and dominating central term is "redemption." That term draws about itself the meaning, presence, and promise of God to Israel which, in her own understanding, was disclosed to her in creation, in historical covenant, and in the interpretation of historical events whereby the fidelity of God to his people was known and celebrated.

The fundamental meaning of grace is the goodness and loving-kindness of God and the activity of this goodness in and toward his creation. Israel knew God in that way, but this knowledge is never specified in the sense of being identified with a term, or a concept, or a single action having an absolute primacy. The uncovenanted, precovenanted, will and disposition that does what it does from within itself (and then "covenants" to secure the reality of the doing), has as its most common names the terms *Chen* and *Hesed. Chen* is God's initiating grace; *Hesed* is faithfulness or loyalty in all covenants and relationships based on *Chen*. The content of these terms shines through such passages as Exodus 33:17–19 and 34:6–7.

A feeling for the form and function of such statements, integral as they are to Israel's understanding of God, of how he manifests, rules, blesses, and intends for his people, indicates that later large categories under which life was divided into life-as-nature and life-as-history are useless for grasping the structure of Israel's faith. It must rather be seen that God is "the Holy One," that all that is is given, and all that happens as event and process is to be related to his faithfulness in mercy and in judgment. This fidelity and presence is manifested in "the glory" and nothing that is or happens is intrinsically incapable of refracting this glory. The "glory of thy people Israel" is the lens in the eye of faith through which all things—natural, personal, social, historical—are beheld. Nebuchadnezzar can be the strange agent of this glory; the glory which "thou hast set *above* the heavens" is also declared *by* the heavens. Nature is not an entity or a process set alongside God and having its own autonomy, its own "insides," its "laws." It is, rather, continuous with the reality of God as Creator. This is not to say that for the man of the Old Testament God is knowable by *Naturwissenschaft*, just as God is not knowable by *Geisteswis-*

*senschaft.* God is made known to man in the matrix of space, time, and matter, which are the substance of that mortal theatre in which God deals with his people in their historical actuality.

These comments about Israel are intended as a background whereby what shall presently be said about the movement of New Testament testimony to Christ and the scope of his grace may be understood both in its Christ-concentration, and in its extent. For if the doctrine of the divine redemption there centered upon Christ is not assessed as moving toward the same spatial largeness as characterized the Old Testament celebration of the "space of the glory" such a movement will continue to be ignored in Christian theology, or rejected, or regarded as marginal or esoteric.

If grace, as witnessed to in the New Testament, is to be proposed in fresh ways of address as actually the will and power of God in Jesus Christ for the redemption of men, and if the actuality of contemporary man's formation-as-man in virtue of his life-conditions and transactions with nature is to be taken seriously, then Christian theology must explicate a doctrine of grace in continuity with the Scripture and in such bold and new reformulations as the reality of grace and its salvatory power demands.

To undertake that task of obedience is a large order placed upon the desk of the theologian, and the task falls with both particular urgency and promise upon all who stand within the Protestant tradition. The urgency does not require much amplification. When a tradition announces that its peculiar contribution to catholic Christendom is its clear and permeating witness to the freedom of God in his grace, and organizes its theological systematic around that proclamation, the urgency is in the tradition itself. And the promise lies in the evangelical insight that made it central there.

But even so tentative an essay as this must specify some practical embarrassments as the task is undertaken. The chief one is this:

the same confessional tradition which has been relentlessly acute
and productive in biblical studies hesitates (particularly in such
theological statements as emanate from its self-conscious confessional assemblies) to introduce the results of such studies into its
theological schematizations and formulations. The same church
whose scholars have contributed so richly to the clarification of
the conditions within which the New Testament was written, the
variety of its focus and terms of witness, the startling fecundity
of its faith-responding speech and the vast reach of its vision and
reference, has permitted highly stylized accents and motifs in the
Scripture to control its present as, in quite a different era in
biblical scholarship, they controlled its past.

With no diminishment in gratitude for the past, and in the
conviction that centeredness upon grace is indeed proper and
obedient, we must reacknowledge with our fathers that formulations must follow the energies of realities, and that theology has
a transbiblical obligation to be exercised in that creative reflection
to which reference has been made. And if such reflection is to be
creative, some responsible risks have to be taken, some realities
and meanings have to be proposed for faith within, but not derived
from, the ever-changing formation of man within the convolutions
and creativities of culture.

There is within the New Testament no single or simple way of
speaking of God and man and grace and history and the natural
world. Indeed, the New Testament witness to God and to Christ
discloses a process, with the Scriptures of Israel back of it and a
variety of world situations around and in front of it, which can
be characterized as a process of fusion, transformation, and
clarification.

Fusion means that elements disclosed in separated episodes are
put together in fresh combinations. Transformation means that
the resultant motif is more than and different from the sum of the
components. Clarification means that what was partial, opalescent,
and potential in components thus fused becomes more full, trans-

parent, and concentrated. That such fusion, transformation, and clarification characterizes the New Testament is here argued; it is not the point at the moment to evaluate that happening.

The community that produced the New Testament did not undertake its task of witness to Christ with a full heart and an empty head. Nor did it fashion its statements with minds that were innocent of the substance, texture, referential opulence, or historical solidity of the terms, images, and symbols of the people of the old covenant. They bore witness to Christ as the center and intention of all these; but the Christ to whom they bore witness was in continuity with the God of Abraham, Isaac, and Jacob. That this witnessing Christocentrism was intended as a modification of the theocentrism of the faith of Israel is a notion that would have been regarded by the writers of the New Testament as both incredible and blasphemous. When the community spoke of Christ's doing they were speaking of God's doing; when they cherished and transmitted Christ's speaking they were reporting what they believed to be an address to them and through them of the reality of God. This faith, this continuity, and this intention was, indeed, generative of a community that knew itself to be constituted by an event that was nothing less than a new form of the God-relationship; but the articulation of that new form at the same time testifies to the old in the very substance of its reportorial and testimonial language.

Form-critical methods in New Testament study have in our time so powerfully intersected with the evaporation of transcendent categories as to produce the current hermeneutical impasse. For the purpose of this discussion it is not necessary to come down with a decision for or against any of the many parties and positions of that effort to forge an ample and correct method of interpretation. I have in another place[1] stated my conviction that the radical either–or's of the academicians are excessively rigid, and achieve their apparent total demolition of opponents by a strange humorlessness about the richness of the

*Beautiful!*

modalities of historical life. Kerygma without narrative leaves
unaccounted for the very substance which made kerygma effective;
and narrative without kerygmatic proclamation leaves unaccounted
for the very evaluation that preserved and cherished the narratives. But there is happy evidence that the more doctrinaire
proponents of various positions in this debate are beginning to be
embarrassed by their departure from sober attention to the multi-
phasic force and form of the Gospel proposal as this proposal
was made to both Jew and Gentile.

> The key to our problem taken as a whole is not the question of the
> historical Jesus as such and in isolation over against the kerygma,
> but the kerygmatic reversion to the narrative form *after* enthusiasm,
> mythological representations and dogmatic reflection had already
> carried the day to the extent illustrated by the primitive Christian
> hymns. Correspondingly, in the case of the mysterious Cosmocrator,
> a dazzling light is reflected back upon him who traverses Palestine
> as a rabbi. How could they revert from glorifying him who was the
> object of preaching to telling the story of him who was himself the
> preacher—and within the framework of the kerygma at that? This
> question is of pre-eminent significance, both historically and theo-
> logically—but Bultmann has not put it. Obviously, he hardly sees it.[2]

Generations of scholarship have noted and specified the huge
variety of the New Testament witness to Christ. And dogmatic
response to that variety has very often been an imposition upon
it of an order dictated by concerns foreign to the data, but creative
of a hierarchy of importance by which the wilderness of the
data could be given the neatness and sequence so satisfying to
system. But the vitality of the variety continues to trouble the
seeming solidity of the system. One tradition begins with the
prophetic announcement in dramatic terms that the time of the
kingly rule of God is imminent; another tradition sets the incomparable evaluation of the event of Christ within the birth stories;
another sets the events it employs for the construction of its
pattern within the vast matrix of "In the beginning was the

Word." It thus organically relates the redemptive grace which is the burden of its new message with the uncovenanted and covenanted grace of God in creation and in Israel's history.

Nor is this variety, including the conceptual magnificence of the Fourth Gospel, an aspect of the testimony to Christ that comes to us only in those literary forms that we know as the Gospels. In the Pauline and other voices of the first century there is a language of testimony, an articulation of vitalities and relations into concatenated forms that reach back historically into Israel's past, grope forward into the future, and impart an eschatological cruciality to the present eon.

Is it possible to speak of this variety in such a way as, on the one hand, to honor the warning against dogmatic "arrangement," and, on the other, to acknowledge that there is movement in this witness, that the referential amplitude is vastly wider in some voices than in others, that the vision of the meaning sweeps in some an arc whose circumference enfolds things near and clear and in others an arc whose axis is "before the foundation of the world" and whose outriding reaches are "... the mystery of his will—a plan for the fullness of time, to unite all things in him, things in heaven and things on earth"?

It is possible not only to remark these differences but also to behold them as differences-in-motion. That motion is clearly not chronological; and efforts to make "high Christology" late and "low Christology" early in the community's recorded experience are clearly illegitimate. If, then, that "motion" was not chronological, how may its nature and direction be designated? It is here proposed that christological momentum may be the most accurate term for what the literature of the New Testament discloses. Differences in the size of the circles of range and reference are clearly in the material, and the types of the rhetoric of celebration which these employ can be noted.

The phrase "rhetoric of celebration" is calculated to break discussion loose from the grip of such language-analysis as would bestow intelligibility and "truth-claim-possibility" upon only such statements as can be shorn of their force-constituting images and reduced to verifiable components. For when theological discourse consents to divest itself of speech appropriate to the modalities appropriate to the historical, and acquiesces in the lust for clarity, intent, purport, and meaning as these take their model from ahistorical operations of the mind, Christian theological discussion will have bowed itself out of the company of significant disciplines.

As biblical and theological scholarship moves toward a more inclusive and precise formulation of the hermeneutical problem, more serious attention is being given to what theological implications inhere in style of speech and forms of rhetoric as these come to us from the earliest Christian communities. The phrase "style of life," common among contemporary ethicists, is a reminder that there is an organic and integral *gestalt* which is back of, down under, and formative of lived-experience and response, and is a force that escapes overly systematic efforts to specify and contain it. When, then, appeal is made to "style" or "type of rhetoric" the intention is not to evade or give a low estimation of such painstaking textual analysis as grounds theological insight. The appeal is rather that we consider whether problems disclosed by analysis and not soluble in terms of analysis alone might be illuminated by such ways of listening as are denoted by the words "style" and "rhetoric." For there is an undilutable momentum, a "blooming" of the language of Christ-testimony, in the New Testament. There is a way of praise and glorification that probes for a largeness of language appropriate to its ultimacy. This intention describes widening circles of meaning, is a living illustration of that embarrassment of purely designative language in the presence of overwhelming encounters and freshly given possibilities. Is it possible to formulate a typology of rhetoric that might both discern and to some degree illustrate patterns in this process? The following is a tentative proposal.

## Rhetoric of Recollection

In this type, the testimony to Christ has its ground in, receives its force from, and takes its direction from the rich and various vocabulary for the hope of Israel. The promises of God are the hope of Israel. These promises, the hope engendered and sustained by them, and the designations in specific terms of how this hope had become incandescent in Jesus Christ constitute a major strand in the New Testament. The terms and images of these promises and of this hope are recollected, used in fresh continuations with recorded teachings and deeds, fused with one another and welded to present events, transformed in many and sometimes strange, sometimes strained ways.

The list of such promise-transmitting and hope-carrying terms is a long one: Son of God, servant of God, royal king, David's son, Priest, suffering witness to the covenant, sorrowing man of the remnant, Lamb of God, Shepherd of Israel, the Word and Wisdom of God, the "glory" of Israel manifest in the "light" to the Gentiles, etc.

This way of testifying-forward by recollecting-backward characterizes many of the words of Jesus. It was a way of opening the mind, shocked by the marvelous deed or the astounding word, to the promise and power already known and attested by Israel. Its momentum toward the cruciality of the moment and the indeterminate possibility of the future is fused within and kerygmatically uncoiled from the inheritance already known—"you know neither the Scriptures nor the power of God!"

The way in which this rhetoric of recollection was worked out is, to be sure, different in the various documents. It is quite clearly the organizing principle of the first chapter of St. Luke's Gospel: the management of the birth narratives is a superb quasi-liturgical prolegomenon to the record about to be entered. The continuation of the testimony in the Acts of the Apostles fashions entire sermons that disclose the same intention.

The Fourth Gospel grounds its particular christological momentum farther back and deep under the historical manifestations in Israel's life, in that beginning which was "the Word." The writer asserts that the Word has always shone in a darkness that has not overcome it, leaps to "a man sent from God," and from the Baptist to the enfleshed Word who is focused presence in humanity of "the glory."

The prologue to the Fourth Gospel is an instance of something that has very often happened in the history of exegesis and in the development of doctrine: a term, or a pericope dominated by a term, may be so closely identified with a particular theological issue that consideration of it apart from that issue becomes difficult. The power of association determines the interpretation.

Writing in 1951, Allan D. Galloway said:

> It is unfortunate that modern theology has always regarded the Logos doctrine primarily as a doctrine of the person of Christ rather than a part of the doctrine of the work of Christ. The two can never be completely separated, of course. And the Logos doctrine is manifestly a doctrine of the person of Christ. But if we interpret it against its background in Paul, we shall see that it is a doctrine of the person of Christ which arose in answer to the problems of interpreting the *work* of Christ to the gentile world. Therefore, in the long run, it is primarily as an assertion of the cosmic significance of the *work* of Christ that we should see it.[3]

It is a responsibility, and a pleasure, to record here my debt to Mr. Galloway's work. While I had, before reading *The Cosmic Christ,* come some distance along the road marked out by the argument of these essays, Mr. Galloway's work was instructive, stimulating, and supportive.

A formal analysis of the structure of St. Paul's proposal of Christ discloses a steady if sometimes allegorical and strained use of the same rhetoric of recollection. One has only to reflect upon the regularity in St. Paul's letters of such connective terms as "Well then," "therefore," "If then," "for this cause." So absolutely is this recollective "connective-tissue" the substance of the point of the address in any section of Paul's letters that responsible preaching about anything the apostle says requires that the verse or pericope be thrust into the entire argument. This process requires nothing less than the recollection of everything he says as the sufficient context for anything he says.

### Rhetoric of Participation and Reenactment

The "model" of this type, if one may substitute a modern way of speaking for an ancient one, is not so much the carrying forward of the past into remembrance in order to interpret the present, as it is an organic process whereby redemption is given in and by participation in that One who is in himself the culmination of a process. If in these days, as one testimony has it, God has spoken to us in the enpersonalized Word, then participation in and vital reenactment of that Word in its earthly career is the model of redemption.

This type of rhetoric proposed that in the actual life, obedience, suffering, death, and resurrection of Jesus Christ is concentrated both the reality of alienation and its conquest by the grace of God. The morphology of this divine-human microcosm is the reality and model of redemption; nothing short of a responding reenactment of the dynamics of it, as these are illuminated and empowered by the Spirit, is the reality of the Christian life.

The morphology of grace "repeats" itself within the morphology of the life called into new being by grace. Professor Amos Wilder puts the matter as follows:

> . . . the gospel is not a history so much as a ritual re-enactment or *mimesis*. The believer did not hear it as a record of the past. With the brotherhood he found himself in the middle of the world-changing transaction of conflict, death and glory. We have here a new speech-form in the profound sense of a new communication of meaning, by which men could live.[4]

The speech of Jesus about the vine and the branches roots this model firmly in the recollected tradition; but in the pastoral counsels recorded in the Epistles this way of redemption is fully and variously filled out. The eloquence and immediacy of this rhetoric of participation and reenactment gains in force when one recognizes that its introduction into apostolic discourse is suggested not by pedagogical-doctrinal concerns but by concrete pastoral situations. The doctrinally crucial statements are evoked by the necessity for the apostle to ground his pastoral counsel; and when, as in the passages we are about to note, the biographical detail is inserted, that insertion is not an end in itself, but en route to an elaboration of the morphology of prevenient grace in Christ.

The significance of this pastoral occasion for the formulation of the doctrine lies not only in the sufficiency of the doctrine to address the situation confronted, but—and this is more important —in the complete naturalness with which, to adduce an instance from Paul, the apostle forges a vast christological statement as alone sufficient to deal with concrete problems in the Philippian community. The last verses of the first chapter report the apostle's concern over the threats to unity and courage among his fellow believers at Philippi. The great christological song in 2:5–11 is but a doxology in Christ whereby the apostle places the moment's trouble in the context of Incarnation, ablation, and exaltation. We are to "have this mind" because this mind *is* ours for the having in the man Jesus. "Have this mind—which you have!" The interchange is a product of that grace whose model is participation and reenactment.

In the third chapter of the same epistle occurs an even more dramatic instance of the same type. The community is to "Beware of those dogs," "the evil-workers," "those who insist upon circumcision." Between the warning and the responding counsel are seven verses of biographical detail about Paul himself. But the point of that detail is only to witness and certify out of the intimate experience of the writer that he has been and continues to be formed in grace by an obedience repetitive of the divine grace. What God does in Christ has a shape; it is an entering into human life, a suffering, a dying, a resurrection from the dead. This lived-out structure of the Christ-deed of grace is identical with the lived-out interior drama of the life of the believer. Faith is participation, and participation is reenactment, and the stages of reenactment are the same as the stages of the Act. "To know him" is not a matter of cognition at a distance or an obedience by affirmation. Knowledge is a gift given to giving one's self over to that renewal of the self which is nothing less than a "resurrection from the dead." Suffering and death, the reality of Christ's life, are actual reenactments within the life of faith.

This grace-from-above, in its power to deal in and by grace with things within and around, is disclosed and illustrated in the final chapter of the Philippian letter. This chapter is a veritable Christology for secularity. The grace of God whereby "Christ Jesus has made me his own" establishes the center. But the center is not the circumference; the circumference of the grace which is redemption is not smaller than that theatre of life and awareness which is the creation. The grace that *came* in enpersonalized Incarnation in Jesus Christ is no other than the grace of God who is Creator, Sustainer, and Law-giver. From the pinnacle of this grace of God, given in the desolation and victory of Christ's immolated life, all things are to be seen, evaluated, used, enjoyed, and made the field of grace. *Therefore*—"whatever is true, whatever is honorable, whatever is just, whatever is pure, whatever is lovely, whatever is gracious, if there is any excellence, if there is anything worthy of praise, think about these things. What you have learned and received and heard and seen in me, do; and the God of peace will be with you" (Phil. 4:8–9).

In Romans 6:1–11 the pattern is almost exactly repeated. The dynamics of sin and grace are presented with the same rhetorical type of discourse. The actuality wrought out by a man in one place becomes the morphology of grace for every man in every place, and the transmission of power is by way of participation-as-reenactment: baptism-burial-raised from the dead. The language of reenactment here takes on a fierce literalness—"For if we have become incorporate with him in a death like his we shall also be one with him in a resurrection like his. If we thus died with Christ we believe that we shall also come to life with him."

When we extend illustration of this type of Christ-grace testimony to the Epistles we find that every centrally operational term of that rich vocabulary receives added relations and meanings. The concept of faith as participating membership "in the body" is so constant and crucial that one is led to hope that the currents of post-Reformation theology and devotion, in the course of which the doctrine of the mystical body was virtually excised from Protestant reflection, might be reconsidered. For any effort to reduce the organic structure of the New Testament language about grace to terms which ignore life in the body of Christ as participation, reenactment, and interchange is so radical an excision as to constitute a mutilation.

## Rhetoric of Cosmic Extension

While our attention in this section will be centered in that strand of testimony that we have called "cosmic extension," it is necessary to refer, however briefly, to that understanding of the scope of the power of God and images appropriate to it which were ready at hand to the Jewish Christians of the first century of the Christian era. The material was there and capable of christological extension because it could not be avoided; it belonged to the substance of God-understanding and nature-understanding in Israel. In his *Inspiration and Revelation in the Old Testament,* H. W. Robinson has the following paragraph:

> The Hebrew vocabulary includes no word equivalent to our term 'Nature.' This is not surprising if by 'Nature' we mean 'The creative and regulative physical power which is conceived of as operating in the physical world and as the immediate cause of all its phenomena.' The only way to render this idea into Hebrew would be to say simply 'God.' We should have to describe a particular physical

activity through anthropomorphic phrases such as the 'voice' of God, heard in the thunder; the 'hand' of God, felt in the pestilence; the 'breath' of God, animating the body of man; the 'wisdom' of God, ultimately conceived as His agent in creation.[5]

Our modern view of nature as by definition not having anything to do with the divine is in complete hiatus with the Old Testament view. There nature comes from God, cannot be apart from God, and is capable of bearing the "glory" of God.[6]

Such a view of God and nature makes completely clear why the redemption of God is celebrated in proleptic visions of a restored nature. For the realm of redemption cannot be conceived as having a lesser magnitude than the realm of creation. The creation as "fallen" is never permitted to exempt its form and creatures and destinies from the great salvation. Professor Allan D. Galloway has written:

> But the Synoptic Gospels do not merely repeat the earlier Jewish insight. Apart from any other considerations, there is this great difference that for the New Testament writers the great redeeming event was no longer a distant future hope, but had already occurred. It had not come fully or finally, but only partially and ambiguously; yet it had become sufficiently actual to transfer their eschatological hopes from the realm of dreaming fantasy to that of present reality. The Messiah had come and already the eyes of the blind were opened and the ears of the deaf unstopped. The lame man leaped as an hart and the dumb sang, and the multitudes were fed on miraculous bread. Whatever the events which lay behind these stories in the early tradition of the church they were sufficiently powerful in their significance to convince the first Christians that the new age had actually come, and only its final fulfillment was still lacking. Already in the Anointed One the things of heaven and the things of earth were joined together.
>
> Something physical, as well as spiritual, had happened in the work of Christ. Indeed these two concepts are not held in the same kind of contrast as they would be now in the twentieth century. Our Lord made a sharp distinction between outward forms and personal faith; but this is a different thing from the contrast between spirit and matter.[7]

As we turn to the Epistles for a type of christological ascription which swings out to cosmic dimensions, we are aware that we are dealing with statements which, in Western Christology at least, have remained marginal, if admitted at all, to the most influential treatises. In the section to follow, we shall indicate the eccentric character of this development and propose some speculations to account for it. But a preliminary task is to face and put into proper perspective two common objections to such attention as shall be given to sections in the letters to the Colossians and the Ephesians where the cosmic type receives fullest statement.

The first objection is the still unsettled problem of authorship of both epistles, and, in the instance of the Colossians, the literary integrity. This objection is legitimate but not crucial. It has greatest weight for those scholars whose purely textual work has alienated them, or kept them from even having been interested in that entire process whereby documents achieve status in a tradition, or in the theological and historical importance of the fact that such status has never been withheld from these letters. The theologian cannot, to be sure, formulate serious statements by scooping up fragments from whatever he finds interesting in the milieu of the early church. But he is also forbidden to permit open questions of a technical nature to dash from his hand sources which have indubitable standing in the tradition, which have from the earliest times been accepted as having apostolic authority, and whose substance is not severable from powerful strands of patristic teaching, preaching, and catechesis.

As systematic theological reflection moves through historical time, it must not only discard biblical literalism (and that battle is far behind us); it must also discard a subtle form of literalistic thinking which persists in what might be called "quantitative literalism." By that I mean a higher or lower regard for the power and implications of a theme according to the frequency of its presentation in the Scripture. The Christian reality is not separable from the Scripture, and it is not identical with or limited to the

Scripture. Theological reflection is in continuity with themes, records, episodes, teachings, etc., as these meet us in Scripture, and has in these its engendering and controlling norm. But hearing the Word and doing theology is an exercise in faithful reflection which, if it is to be intelligible, must partake of the dynamism of all historical, cultural, and experiential life. In the evolution of man's biological form and capabilities across the millennia of time, nature probed in an infinite virtuosity of effort the possibility for higher forms—some abortive, some rich with phyla that led to higher forms. As from one strand among the very many, and that one not in its earlier stages notably different from others, nature fashioned the progenitors of man. So the Christologies that emerged in the first several centuries, while certainly not "wrong," do not in their number or structure actualize all the potentialities that lie resident within the magnificent doxological witness of the community to Christ.

Theology always, to transform a statement of Goethe, in the need of the moment seizes that which shall serve and bless it. Such a strand of early witness to Christ is here alluded to under the phrase "cosmic extension." That this theme is in the New Testament a tentative, probing theme, some expressions of which seem to have been evoked by the gnostic, or another, heresy, that the theme has not been worked out with the systematic fullness that characterizes clearer and more amply attested christological images and ascriptions—all of this must be acknowledged. But it must also be insisted that the theme is a legitimate accent in the rhetoric of the earliest community, that its referential roots in the Scripture are deep, that confessional or other solid continuities dare not impose impediments to its scrutiny. The contours of need and interest in the long life of the people of God have time after time found contours of disclosure in the Scripture. St. Augustine's treatise on the Holy Trinity is no less admirable because we know the cultural crises that evoked it and gave to it the particular analogical form it has.

The implications that are resident within the preceding paragraph are most likely to be seized upon by New Testament scholars whose hermeneutical principles are (a) unchanged by the exposure of the community-forming and preaching character of the New Testament documents and, (b) would restrict theological development to changing forms of statement believed identical with the "intention" of the writer and the text.

The development of the science and art of interpretation has, however, moved through several stages, and has now come to a way of hearing and understanding a text which provides not only a fresh encounter with the old discipline of biblical theology but also a creative way to move from biblical theology to the ever-new tasks of systematic theology.

The several stages through which hermeneutical inquiry has moved are most generally designated as a hermeneutics of symbolical language, a hermeneutics of existential phenomenology, and a hermeneutics of structure. This last model relies mainly on the affirmation that language, before being a process or an event, is a system, and that this system is not established at the level of the speaker's consciousness, but at a lower level, that of the structural unconscious.

This third phase actually stops all legitimate efforts to use biblical texts for constructive theological efforts. For the

> . . . idea that language is a closed system of signs within which each element merely refers to other elements of the system, excludes the claim of hermeneutics to reach beyond the "sense"—as the immanent content of the text—to its "reference," i.e., to what it says *about* the world. For structuralism, language does not refer to anything outside of itself, it constitutes a world for itself. Not only the reference of the text to an external world, but also its connections to an author who *intended* it and to a reader who *interprets* it are excluded by structuralism."[8]

The business of hermeneutics is presently in a vigorous shambles. This is so largely because of the adamant and humorless way in which each position has pounded itself into meaningless pulp by its own narrowness. In the same essay to which reference has been made (in note 8), Professor Ricoeur feels his way toward a method of interpretation of texts which seems to me most fully appropriate to the way the community of faith bore witness in the words of Scripture, most rich in that potential for hearing and obedience which has in fact been the force of biblical speech for centuries, and most congruent with that "living Word" to which the church gives proper praise.

The kind of hermeneutics which I now favor starts from the recognition of the objective meaning of the text as distinctive from the subjective intention of the author. This objective meaning is not something hidden behind the text. Rather it is a requirement addressed to the reader. The interpretation accordingly is a kind of obedience in this injunction starting from the text. The concept of "hermeneutical circle" is not ruled out by this shift within hermeneutics. Instead it is formulated in new terms. It does not proceed so much from an intersubjective relation linking the subjectivity of the author and the subjectivity of the reader as from a connection between two discourses, the discourse of the text and the discourse of the interpretation. This connection means that what has to be interpreted in a text is what it says and what it speaks about, i.e., the kind of world which it opens up or discloses; and the final act of "appropriation" is less the projection of one's own prejudices into the text than the "fusion of horizons"—to speak like Hans-Georg Gadamer—which occurs when the world of the reader and the world of the text merge into one another.

This shift within hermeneutics from a "romanticist" trend to a more "objectivist" trend is the result of this long travel through structuralism. At the same time, I had to depart from my previous definition of hermeneutics as the interpretation of symbolic language. Now I should tend to relate hermeneutics to the specific problems raised by the translation of the objective meaning of written language into the personal act of speaking which a moment ago I called appropriation. In that way, the broader question, What is it to interpret a text? tends to replace the initial question, What is it to interpret symbolic language? The connection between my first definition and the new emerging definition remains an unsolved problem for me. . . .[9]

The foregoing provides a way of replying to any who would stop all current reflection about the reality of the cosmos in the determination of God by saying of, for instance, my statements about the "cosmic" Christology of Colossians 1, that "this is not what the writer intended!"

It is not, I think, what the writer "intended"; for the writer did not look out upon a world as an organism, as an evolutionary ecosystem. The writer was not an enthusiastic proleptic Teilhard de Chardin, or a Darwin, or a Niels Bohr. But the writer does, from a faith that affirms the grace of God the Creator and the incarnated grace of God the Redeemer and the present working of God the Sanctifier, enfold within his vision of the new evolution a "horizon" of meaning and hope that cannot stop short of "all things." "Intention" is no adequate guide for biblical hermeneutics; to *see the world* as the text speaks of it is a constructive theological enterprise that must not be dismissed out of hand by the too easy demonstration that meanings in an ancient context are not identical with meanings in a present context.

The second objection to extensive theological reflection based upon the rhetoric of cosmic extension arises most commonly from those scholars who are aware of the gnostic influence against which the "cosmical" passages from the Colossians are likely directed, and who, while admitting the scanty state of accurate knowledge of gnosticism, feel that these verses should be regarded as marginal to any theological employment. While the caution urged by such a position must be attended to, other facts have balancing weight. There is, first of all, the fact that the christological scope of these verses is not esoteric within the body of the Epistles. The organic nature of the language and of the concepts is continuous with, although bold extensions of, central and repeated celebrations of the role and rule and scope of Christ's presence and power. Secondly, the occasion for the statements—

and this regardless of how clear or how problematical the gnostic incitement of that may be assessed—has really little to do with the substance of the argument. Occasions may explain why something is said as it is said to those to whom it is said. But clarity about occasions does not validate or invalidate substance.

If then it is granted that the gnostic heresy was probably the occasion for raising the issue of the scope of Christ's redemptive reign, and if our knowledge about the peculiar vocabulary of gnosticism provides the clue to the language of some parts of the epistles to the Colossians and the Ephesians, some kind of systematic reply was required, and these epistles supply it. The reply is clear, unambiguous, and has a magnitude that matches the size of the issue. Galloway has a summary of the reply:

> The implications of this teaching [gnosticism] places a limit on the work of Christ. It says in effect: Christ has redeemed us from Satan and the spirits of the lower air. But we are still subject to the elemental powers beyond that. In other words, some doubt had arisen whether Christ's work really was cosmic in its scope. [Note the implication of this heresy: That if it was thus limited, then something further was required for our complete redemption.][10]

The essence of the answer is the assertion that the work of Christ is universally effective for all creation. The demonic powers in all parts of the universe have been "disarmed" by him (Colossians 2:15):

> The argument runs as follows: Christ is eternally preexistent (Col. 1:17), therefore he has power over eternal spheres. He is the image of the Father (Col. 1:15), and this insures his supremacy over all angels and powers. He was actually the divine agent in the creation of all these things (Col. 1:15–16). Therefore, his redeeming work which has been declared $\dot{\epsilon}\nu\ \pi\acute{a}\sigma\eta\ \kappa\tau\acute{\iota}\sigma\epsilon\iota\ \tau\hat{\eta}\ \dot{\upsilon}\pi\grave{o}\ \tau\grave{o}\nu\ o\dot{\upsilon}\rho\alpha\nu o\nu$ is unlimited in its efficacy. In him God "reconciles all things to himself, whether on earth or in heaven, through him alone" (Col. 1:20).[11]

To appreciate what has been called a type of christological teaching that employs a "rhetoric of cosmic extension" we should have the entire pericope before us:

He rescued us from the domain of darkness and brought us away into the kingdom of his dear Son, in whom our release is secured and our sins forgiven. He is the image of the invisible God; his is the primacy over all created things. In him everything in heaven and on earth was created, not only things visible but also the invisible orders of thrones, sovereignties, authorities, and powers: the whole universe has been created through him and for him. And he exists before everything, and all things are held together in him. He is, moreover, the head of the body, the church. He is its origin, the first to return from the dead, to be in all things alone supreme. For in him the complete being of God, by God's own choice, came to dwell. Through him God chose to reconcile the whole universe to himself, making peace through the shedding of his blood upon the cross—to reconcile all things, whether on earth or in heaven, through him alone (Col. 1:13–20).

How the scope of this claim and its language of absolute inclusiveness bears upon the issues of grace and nature, grace and history, grace and the problematic of the modern self is to be the matter for later discussion. What is required here is that we permit this christological affirmation to question, profoundly modify, and open to fresh dimensions of interpretation types of christological thought which have a less broad reference. For the range and interior resonance of this doxological theology is astounding. Nothing less than the vast orbits of natural structure and of historical process and mystery constitute the far-circling of it. Even in these times, when events have tightened human thought around the tormented center of the meaning of personal existence, and when, consequently, the church's Christology has focused about a radically existentialist interpretation of Christ the Redeemer, this polyphonic hymn to the scope and energy of the divine redemption sounds to haunt the church's mind.

When in the doxology that marks the long and tortuous argument in the letter to the Romans, St. Paul gathers up the elements that enter into his reflections about the destiny of Israel under the fresh manifestation of God in the Gospel of Christ, the apostle does not really solve the problem. The continuing history of this argument in the career of the church attests that. He thrusts the insoluble into the indisputable. The recalcitrant historical fact is that ". . . God has consigned all men to disobedience, that he may have mercy upon all." The doxology that follows is the language of startled praise, a rhetoric of wonder before God's mercy and the puzzle of history, which has the same magnificence as characterizes the Colossians rhetoric about grace and nature.

> O depth of wealth, wisdom, and knowledge in God! How unsearchable his judgments, how untraceable his ways! Who knows the mind of the Lord? Who has been his counsellor? Who has ever made a gift to him, to receive a gift in return? Source, Guide, and Goal of all that is—to him be glory for ever! Amen (NEB).

The eighth chapter of Romans is another occasion in which we see the conceptually insoluble gathered into a doxological affirmation in which elements that are resistant to logical penetration are fused together. The statement in verse 28 that the spirit ". . . pleads for God's people in God's own way—and cooperates for good with those who love God," is not a logical outcome of the mighty themes of the chapter. It is rather a remembering at the end of the insoluble that only the unmerited fact that he who "did not spare his own Son" is One who in that action is to be trusted to "lavish upon us all he has to give." Then follows, not a fresh attack upon the issue, but a doxological celebration of the God who having done the central action will not ultimately have his love either frustrated or bounded by whatever meaninglessness persists in natural structures, or historical mysteries.

> . . . and yet, in spite of all, overwhelming victory is ours through him who loved us. For I am convinced that there is nothing in death or life, in the realm of spirits or superhuman powers, in the world as it is or the world as it shall be, in the forces of the universe, in heights or depths—nothing in all creation that can separate us from the love of God in Christ Jesus our Lord (Rom 8:37–39 NEB).

These instances from the Pauline manner and speech are not proposed as supportive of the substance of the Colossians hymn in 1:15–20, but as evidences that <u>the scope of the passage shall</u> <u>not be thought marginal either to the apostle's thought</u> and range <u>or to the imperial christological momentum of which he is in</u> other contexts capable. The entire axis from the "invisible God" to the repeated "all things" is unbroken. The reality of that Godly action, Christ, is declared present in, the agent of, and the goal and meaning of literally all that is. The relational prepositions "in" him, "through" him, "for" him are here constitutive of a christological claim that stretches out endlessly in time, space, and effectual force. The reality of Christ as the focal point for world and life meaning is sunk back into the "invisible God," is that energy whereby "all things hold together," and is proposed forward into the yet uncut pages of historical life as God's purpose and power "to reconcile to himself all things."

The "systematic" of this energy as it may be proposed as conceptually apposite to our time with its radically new understanding of nature and its excruciatingly acute historical consciousness, is a task that must be taken up in following pages. But in order that the clarity of the claim shall not rest upon too narrow a formulation in the New Testament witness, the language of another document must be heard.

The salutation to the letter to the Ephesians, as in every Pauline or probable Pauline epistle, fuses into a unity what older dogmatic treatises differentiated by the terms "created" and "uncreated" grace. But grace is single. Its source is "God the Father," its historical agent and embodiment is "the Lord Jesus Christ," and its gift and work is "grace to you and peace" (in II Timothy, "grace, mercy, and peace").

To relate style of speech to the task of understanding is an often neglected component of exegesis. Verses 2–14 in the first chapter of Ephesians is a passage whose very structure demands that this component be considered as somewhat more than an idiosyncrasy of interpretation favored by those peculiar persons who attend to rhetoric as an art. The sheer fecundity of the reality of grace in these verses creates a syntax and a diction to serve its abundance, and a rhetoric to resonate to its richness in unity. The concatenation of phrases, as each within the ordering mind of the writer begets clauses to amplify its reverence, is astounding even for one accustomed to and sometimes impatient with the Pauline style. The English translations commonly break up the rushing momentum of the Greek text, but such a convenience does little to check the felt unfolding of the single massive fact of grace as it multiplies celebrative clauses to adore and proclaim the mystery.

> Peace to you and peace from God our Father and the Lord Jesus Christ. Praise be to God and Father of our Lord Jesus Christ, who has bestowed on us in Christ every spiritual blessing in the heavenly realm. In Christ he chose us before the world was founded, to be dedicated, to be without blemish in his sight, to be full of love; and he destined us—such was his will and pleasure—to be accepted as his sons through Jesus Christ, in order that the glory of his gracious gift, so graciously bestowed on us in his Beloved, might rebound to his praise. For in Christ our release is secured and our sins are forgiven through the shedding of his blood. Therein lies the richness of God's free grace lavished upon us, imparting full wisdom and insight. He has made known to us his hidden purpose—such was his will and pleasure determined beforehand in Christ—to be put into effect when the time was ripe: namely, that the universe, all in heaven and on earth, might be brought into a unity in Christ. . . . In Christ indeed we have been given our share in the heritage, as we decreed in his design whose purpose is everywhere at work. For it was his will that we, who were the first to set our hope on Christ, should cause his glory to be praised. And you, too, when you had heard the message of the truth, the good news of your salvation, and had believed it, because incorporate in Christ, and received the seal of the promised Holy Spirit; and that Spirit is the pledge that we shall enter upon our heritage, when God has redeemed what is his own, to his praise and glory (Eph. 1:2–14 NEB).

The subject of the pericope is God. The substance of the affirmations is the work of Christ. The intention of that work is to the "purpose" and "counsel" of God's "will" and "pleasure." The theatre of the action is "when the time was ripe." The *telos* is "that the universe, all in heaven and on earth, might be brought into a unity in Christ." And the leitmotif of the passage, which twice gathers all together upon a plateau of praise, breaks loose again to magnify and clarify the action in fresh ascription, and comes to its target and summation in the third repetition—"to the praise of his glory."

The manner and the matter are one. The graciousness of the structured strophes seem to form their sonorous rhythms from the awesome grace they declare. If the phrase "praise of his glory" seems to modern ears too vaporous to control the great song, that fault lies in us and not in the phrase. If the clear, powerful, absolute meaning of "the glory" strikes no comprehending fire there may be some relation between that failure and the apostle's later word in the fourth chapter where we read:

> This then is my word to you, and I urge it upon you in the Lord's name. Give up living like pagans with their good-for-nothing notions. Their wits are beclouded, they are strangers to the life that is in God, because ignorance prevails among them and their minds have grown hard as stone (Eph. 4: 17–19).

The implicit Christology of this hymn to grace goes in unbroken sequence from the purpose of God "who has bestowed on us in Christ every spiritual blessing in the heavenly realms" to those communities in concrete historical places where men by the Holy Spirit have "heard the word of truth" and by faith live on acknowledging life "in all insight and mystery." This acknowledging community is the body of Christ who is its head. When, later, a conceptualization of the scope of grace was compelled to give dogmatic precision to these organic images of the energy of grace operating in so wide a range, nothing short of the dogma of the Holy Trinity was adequate to set it forth.

We began this section with the assertion that there are within the New Testament types of rhetoric which can be specified, and that such a specification is useful for correction in view of a dogmatic tradition that has not always attended with equal gravity to each of them. It is now necessary to look at several "moments" in the development of the doctrine of grace and see something of the persistence and proportion of these types in that long career.

In the following chapter I shall describe and emphasize a particular strand of the developing doctrine of grace. The intention is to restore a proportion, not to establish a dominance. Such reflection upon the rich and various elements, movements, leading motifs, and receding interests is a constant task of historians of dogma. Indeed, the greatest contribution of this discipline to constructive theology may be that it engages in such reflection, over and over again, pondering the long story from the perspective of each moment in the church's life. Such reflection discloses how intimately related are the thoughts in men's minds and the circumstances of their bodies. Out of this plenitude of possibility a time draws forward now this, now that. It thrusts one aspect of a manifold theme aggressively forward and permits other aspects, equally venerable and well attested, to fall into the background.

Every historian of doctrine has observed that the development of Christian thought is not of equal force and creativity along an entire front. Thought does not move like a wave at full crest. Its movement is rather like that of a slow incoming tide that reaches forward along an uneven beach, pushing forward into low places with long probing fingers. These low-lying or mounded contours are what they are by the working of historical forces which it is the task of research to isolate and describe. The political involvements of a particular people at a particular time in a particular place, the emergence of a single strong person to a position of leadership, a theological position stressed into dominance by a chance congruity of that doctrine with a regnant political position—these and a hundred other influences have a part in the shaping of the undulating life of doctrinal development.

Although, to be sure, there are those who resist the admission of such fortuitous forces as an embarrassing modification of the presidency of the Holy Spirit over the thoughts and practice of the church, such resistance must finally give way before the facts. Nor is this acknowledgment of historical force an abandonment of the integrity of Christian doctrine in its development, or a dismissal of the working of the Spirit. It is rather the coming to effective maturity in historical consciousness of what it really means to say that God discloses his will in history, that the Word really becomes flesh, that the Word of God and the word, and works, and always mixed intentions and protestations of men, exist in a mortal relationship.

If in the pages to follow we shall be selectively attentive to a few figures in the history of doctrine, or stress a single theme as it sounds in concert or even dissonance with others, the intention of the essay must be the defense of the practice. If, quietly present but available within the story of Christian thought there is a christological pattern that has very special power for the life of both faith and culture in this moment, it is both right and good to draw it forth and propose it for reflection.

# 3.

# Some Crucial Moments in
# Ecumenical Christology

Between the material to which we have thus far been attending
and the constructive sections to follow, the present chapter has a
clear and urgent task: to recognize that the traditional scope of
christological understanding is under pressure to achieve vaster
amplitude in virtue of contemporary man's apprehension of the
world-as-nature, and further, to inquire if the doctrine of grace
does not also require a way of proclamation which shall be correlative with new self- and world-understanding. In order to give
sequence and concreteness to my reflections on these matters I
shall recapitulate the theological course whereby I came to enter-
tain them. After some years of participation in Faith and Order
dialogue one's mind becomes aware of a triple process at work:
confidence in the comprehensiveness of all theological formulations is relativized; motivation toward fresh forms of theological
discourse, in recognition of powerful cultural changes, is ener-
gized; and conviction about the enduring and incomparable realities of the Christian faith is solidified.

In such a situation one learns to be wary of sentences which
begin, "There is only one way . . . ," or "The central and persisting
teaching of the church (on this or that topic) is clear . . . ," or
"From the earliest times Jesus has been regarded as . . . ," etc. The
christological ascriptions in both New Testament and theological
reflection resist report under any general statement that can claim
ecumenical plenitude or common authority.

## The East—The Pantocrator

It was the heightened participation of Orthodoxy in the conversations of Faith and Order which first turned my attention to aspects of New Testament language about the grace and the Lordship of Christ which, muted or ignored in entire ranges of Western Christology, have been enormously formative of both theological position and piety in the churches of the East.

If one would analyze to its roots the theological excitement and embarrassment that has occurred within ecumenical encounters because of Orthodox participation one must be careful not to stop at surface factors. Almost a thousand years of theological, ecclesiastical, even personal alienations have begotten a strangeness that proclaims itself in personal bearing, liturgical forms, ceremonial mores, exegetical style, etc. But underneath and absolutely pervasive of the two styles, Eastern and Western, is a different way of speaking about the work of Christ. In the West that work is centered upon redemption from sin; in the East it is centered upon the divinization of man. In the West the doctrine central to that work is atonement; in the East the central doctrine is participation, illumination, reenactment, and transformation. In the West the work of Christ is spoken of chiefly as restoration; in the East the work is reunification. The Western *Savior* is the Eastern *Pantocrator*. The Western *corpus* is the Eastern *Christus Rex*. The Western representation of Christ is Dürer, Grünewald, Rembrandt, Roualt, and a thousand others who center upon the oblation in the passion of Christ. These are matched in the East by the iconography in mosaic, in fresco, and in panel-icon by the known and unknown artists, Byzantine, Russian, and others in which the serene and cosmos-ruling Christ is acknowledged in the heroism of the figures of the saints. The reality of this heroism is not different in the two, but the style and visage and mien of the figures is almost totally different. In the West these figures speak of a rescue from particular forms of lostness—sin and aberration. In the East this rescue is ontologically total; the realization of restored being bestowed by the transformation of grace is manifest in the strong docility, the passionless visage of absolute serenity. Since Harnack, who understood this "stillness" as death, this docility as debility, and this serenity as a defect in personal identity, the West has not known how to understand energy in any form or attitude save motion and activity.

Two paragraphs, the first elaborating the Johannine life-mingling participation in Christ, the second elaborating the theme of cosmic harmony in virtue of the whole creation as brought within the effectual compass of redemption, are here selected. Both are from St. Gregory of Nyssa, and both illuminate the differences in East and West to which we have alluded.

> Let no one accuse us of seeing two Christs or two Lords in the one Savior. But God the Son, who is God by nature, Lord of the universe, King of all creation, the Maker of all that exists and the Restorer of what has fallen, has not only not deprived our fallen nature of communion with Him, but in His great bounty He has deigned even to receive it again into life. But He is Life. Therefore, at the end of centuries, when our wickedness had reached its height, then in order that the remedy might be applied to all that was diseased, He united (lit., "mingled") Himself with our lowly human nature, He assumed man in Himself and Himself became man. He explains this to His disciples: "Ye in Me, and I in you" (John 14:20). By this union He made man what He Himself was. He was the Most High; lowly man was now elevated. For He who was the Most High had not need of being elevated. The Word was already Christ and Lord.[1]

> Since He is in all, He takes into Himself all who are united with Him by the participation of His body; He makes them all members of His body, in such wise that the many members are but one body. Having thus united us with Himself and Himself with us, and having become one with us in all things, He makes His own all that is ours. But the greatest of all our goods is submission to God, which brings all creation into harmony. Then every knee shall bend in heaven, on earth, and under the earth, and every tongue shall confess that Jesus Christ is Lord (Phil. 2:10). Thus all creation becomes one body, all are grafted one upon the other, and Christ

speaks of the submission of His body to the Father as His own submission.[2]

What is remarkable in that paragraph, so characteristic of Orthodoxy, is the way in which the confession that *Jesus Christ is the Lord* gathers about itself images of the divine energy. This gathering, incohering divine energy is testified in the strongly active verbs—he *takes into himself,* he *makes them members,* he *makes his own all that is ours.* The starting point of this theology, as had been remarked and carefully worked out by Professor Charles Moeller, is the efficacious and divinizing presence of Christ in the world and in the church. The classic aphorism in Greek patristic theology asserts:

> Whoever is not assumed is not saved. . . . This doctrine, absolutely common to the whole Christian Church has taken a particular form in the theology of Gregory Palamas, who has had great prominence in the Orthodox tradition since the XV Century. His distinction between the essence and the divine created energies is probably unfamiliar to us. . . . What interests us here is the meaning this distinction takes on in the theology of grace. The choice of terms "uncreated energies" stresses that God reveals himself by acting, which excludes all "passion" from God; but as the energies are "uncreated" there can be no question of making them the fruit of man's merit in any way at all.[3]

Gregory Palamas (1296–1359), bishop and saint in the Orthodox Church, was initiator and expounder of the famous distinction between God's being and his energy or operation. He rejected the Western explanations based on the idea of grace as created and supernatural.[4] Energy, fusion, concorporeal presence—such notions, so common in Orthodoxy, can be understood in their operational force only when we listen to them in an extended passage from Palamas.

> Since the Son of God, through his inconceivable love for man has not only united his divine hypostasis to our nature, and taking a living body and a soul endowed with intelligence, appeared upon earth and lived among men, but even, O wondrous miracle, unites

himself to human hypostases, and fusing himself with each believer by communion of his sacred Body, becomes concorporeal with us and makes us a temple of the whole divinity, for the plentitude of the divinity dwells corporally in Him (Col., II, 9), how does He not enlighten, by surrounding them with light of those who participate in it worthily, as He enlightened even the body of the disciples on Thabor? Then, indeed, this Body possessing the source of the light of grace was not yet fused with our bodies; He enlightened from without those who approached worthily and sent light into their souls through their bodily eyes. But today He is fused with us, He lives within us, and naturally enlightens our soul from within. . . . Only one can see God . . . Christ. We must be united to Christ—and with what an intimate union!—in order to see God.[5]

The foregoing excursion into what is to Western ears an archaic style of christological speech, and the confidence that it will sound exotic to Western ears, is a deliberate tactic. The risk, of course, is great: such a vocabulary for man's gracious God-relation through Christ will likely turn off as many readers as it turns on. But the risk must be taken. For a Christology of the total cosmos with the force and the scope necessary to constitute Christian illumination of Western man's absurd and suicidal operations with nature is not a prominent or even popularly accepted strand within the churches of the West. If one recalls that catholic tradition does indeed include such a possibility, and if his own attachment to it is to escape the charge of idiosyncrasy, then he cannot do other than specify, explicate, and defend. To that end let us listen to a church father in whom the tradition to which we are appealing is strong and clear.[6]

Irenaeus (c. 130–202) relates God and man and grace and nature in a lively way. His explication of the faith is like a complex circuit in a radio receiving set: the wires are all there, all in order, and every connection firmly soldered. But this maze becomes functional for faith, glows with life and clarity, only when plugged in, i.e., admitted to thought via participation! In the Cathedral of the Holy Trinity at Zagorsk, Russia, during the Feast of the Dor-

mition, standing for hours amidst the prayers of the faithful before
the iconostasis with its Anton Rubleff icons—literal presences of
the "mighty cloud of witnesses"—I came to understand a mode of
Christ's reality that shattered assumptions about Western christological comprehensiveness and beckoned toward partly forgotten
dimensions of catholic Christology.

Irenaeus is chosen for detailed discussion for three reasons: (a)
of all the early theologians he most fully worked out a systematic,
biblically derived exposition of God's grace and man's experience
of the world-as-nature; (b) because his christological images were
fashioned in opposition to gnostic dualism and because ever-
renewed forms of that heresy have been a steady accompaniment
to the course of catholic Christology, Irenaeus's "model" has a
startling potential for our time; (c) the doctrine of grace as elaborated by Irenaeus invites the mind to stand within a rich and
neglected mode of thought, and from that position conceive afresh
how the reality of God's grace may be discerned and celebrated
within a desacralized culture.

Let us start with Irenaeus and gnosticism.

The gnostics, pondering the problem of the role of Christ in
the riddle of the universe, found the Christian faith in its apostolic
form too simple. They undertook to give a more complex and
subtle analysis of how the grace of God could be related to the
"graceless space" between the realms of creation and redemption.
This reply, in most general categories, took two forms.

The first form, usually ascribed to Valentinus, postulated a hierarchy of beings who in their totality constitute the Fullness, or
Pleroma, of the deity. Those of the lowest order had departed from
the bright world above and brought into being the material universe. And from this universe gnosticism assumed, in continuity
with a Plotinian extension of Platonic notions, that it is the goal
of true wisdom (*gnosis*) to escape.

The second form of gnostic teaching is in the form of a dualism
which explains the ambiguities of mortal existence by telling of a

conflict between two independent powers, good and evil, or perhaps merely perfect and imperfect. This is Marcionite gnosticism. The proposed way of escape is not merely contemplative; it requires moral athleticism. The world has to be repudiated, despised. This despisal could take the form of ascetical denigration of the physical, or a kind of contemptuousness toward and indulgence of the body. In either case the point was clear: only the higher order mattered; the body was not redeemable. Not even a lesser deity could enter into human nature.

Thus, catholic Christology was repudiated. Gnosticism was an occult form of religion within which nature and grace could not be spoken of together. They mutually excluded each other. While the Irenaean refutation has profoundly intellectual and biblical argument as its support, the style of it, because Irenaeus was a bishop and responsible for saving men from the seductions of a vastly appealing esoteric religion, is pastoral and homiletical. This argument may be detailed as follows: [7]

There is *one* creation, not two; there is one source of all things, not many. The "hands" of God in creation are the *Law* and the *Spirit*. They are uncreated: they belong to the Creator and are active in all creation. God and his creating "hands" are inseparable; it is impossible to penetrate into this "mystery" and find the point of their creation.

The Son is revealed in Jesus Christ but does not originate in Jesus Christ. Therefore it is not correct to argue that belief in him could only come with the Incarnation, "The Word was in the beginning with God." He is (for us) in the Incarnation; there we see him. But he is before the creation of the world.

When man was created he was created through the Son and in the Son and is to reach his destiny in the Son. By this insistence, which characterized early Christian thought, creation and redemption, nature and grace, are formally kept together in a way which, when broken, leads to literally endless theological confusion.

Irenaeus, on the contrary, holds that everything is created in the

Son, and thus secures a theological way to hold nature and grace together. The Word in which all is created is the same *Verbum* which became flesh in Christ. This makes it possible to go from the revelation of God in the Son to a corollary and further revelation of the Father in nature. This is not a "natural theology" in the sense that God is disclosed in nature without the revelation in the Son; but it is a *theology for* nature in the inevitable sense that the hand of God the Creator, which is the hand of the Son, should be seen, following the Incarnation, also in nature.

Just as it is the characteristic of God to create, it is characteristic of man that he is created. He is made, he not simply *is*. His ontology is a resultant of a decisive action: and his "isness" is not a static ontological being but a becoming. He increases. These two, that he is and that he grows, are one reality seen from two different aspects.

Irenaeus regards all life—man's life in solitude and fellowship, in history, and in the life of nature—as in the hands of God. Death is a lost connection with God. By this refusal to adopt a matter-spirit dualism, by keeping together in God all aspects of the creation, Irenaeus held together in his understanding natural life and the Spirit, creation and the sacraments, man's body and his communion with God.

Adam, Irenaeus says, was created by God in God's *Imago and Simultudo,* and was put into God's creation by the same God who sent Christ into the world. Like Paul, Irenaeus plays out the strong contrast between Adam and Christ. But whereas in the Western theology prevailing after Irenaeus the fall of Adam was stressed almost exclusively, Irenaeus fastens attention upon what Adam was created *for,* which is to live, body and soul, in accordance with God's will. By virtue of this accent upon the possible divine intention for man, what is stressed between Adam and Christ is not their separation but their connection.

Christ was the pattern upon which God created man. Christ is the man about to be—the *Homo futurus.* While all things were being formed Christ was in the mind of God, and all things have within themselves this intention: "For this reason the Son also appeared in the fullness of time to show how the copy resembles him."

Adam as a child is the dramatic figure Irenaeus uses to give concreteness to his interpretation. For man, to be unsaved means to remain undeveloped; salvation is maturation and fulfillment. Christ is called and is man's Savior because in him man is shown what maturation is, is called to be nurtured into it, and to grow up into the form of the Son. The healthy, newborn child, says Irenaeus, while unable to talk, possesses every likelihood of becoming able to do so. An injury, to be sure, may prevent the development. And this is the situation of Adam in the world. He is a child, created in the image of God. That he lacks something is not due to sin. No injury has yet happened to the child. Uninjured, he is yet a child, he does not realize what he is yet to be. All the while, however, there is already in creation one who is the full image of God, the Son.

A second influential focus in the teaching of Irenaeus is the large place he gives to the New Testament notion of *anakephaliosis* (recapitulation), and the quite systematic extension it receives in his hands. In this treatment, the parallel, contrast, and connection of the two Adams is central; but a way of thinking about the relation of God, the grace of God, and man's condition as a part of the natural world does not remain confined within the terms of the image. What begins as a "process-soteriology" originated by grace and fulfilled in recapitulation, participation, and reenactment unfolds into something approaching a Christian ontology.

Father E. Mersch describes Irenaeus's use of the term *anakephaliosis* as follows:

By the word recapitulation as applied to Christ Irenaeus means a sort of recommencement in the opposite direction by which God, reversing, as it were, the process whereby sin infected the earth, gathers together and reunites all creation, including matter, but especially man, in a new economy of salvation. He gathers up His entire work from the beginning, to purify and sanctify it in His Incarnate Son, who in turn becomes for us a second stock and a second Adam. In Him, the first Adam and all his posterity are healed; the evil effects of disobedience are destroyed and as it were reversed by their contraries. Man recovers the holiness which was his at the beginning and he is divinized by union with the God from whom he came. As we see, the term presents many meanings: a resume, a taking up of all since the beginning, a recommencement, a return to the source, restoration, reorganization and incorporation under one Head. But these meanings are all related; in spite of their diversity they fit into one another, and even when expressed singly each one suggests all the others.[8]

What is remarkable in this teaching is the way Christ and Adam are so related as to do justice to both difference and bond, to what is wrong and to what is right. Irenaeus clearly foresees what later Trinitarian formulations had to work out in detail: God is over all things as the Word; God is in all things as the spirit who cries "Abba, Father" and forms man in the image of God.

It is instructive to observe that some insights, muffled or forgotten in formal theology, may persist in the liturgies of the church. Irenaeus's "recapitulation" image is a case in point. Still today the powerful image of Christ's active recapitulation of Adam's fateful choice survives in the Lenten Preface to the Holy Communion. "It is truly meet, right, and salutory, that we should at all times and in all places, give thanks unto Thee, O Lord, Holy Father, Almighty, Everlasting God: Who on the tree of the cross didst give salvation unto mankind, that whence death arose, thence life also might rise again; and that he (Satan) who by a tree once overcame (the tree in Eden), might likewise by a Tree (the cross) be overcome. . . ."[9]

While, to be sure, the constant claim of Irenaeus that the orbit of the salvatory work of Christ is universal in scope was a claim which was probably evoked from him by the universalist speculations of gnosticism, the warrant for the teaching is clearly rooted

in the New Testament. The disposition of some historians of doctrine to regard Irenaeus as idiosyncratic is manifestly a Western
prejudice. It is significant that the more deeply the contemporary
church searches her tradition for a christological understanding
appropriate in formal and substantial largeness to contemporary
nature-knowledge and its resultant technology, the more concentrated is her attention to this father. A study of the investigations
into patristic theology which have attended the efforts of the
Roman Church during Vatican Council II, and the deepening
efforts of Faith and Order studies to relate Christ, church, and
world supplies clear evidence of such reawakened attention.[10]

Near the beginning of the treatise *Against the Heretics* is a long
passage that is quoted here because it illustrates how the idea of a
"recapitulation" operates as a kind of hub from which the spokes
of a very full confession of faith extend. These elaborations are
bound together by the encircling rim, and describe a pattern which
is later spoken of in Roman theology as the Mystical Body, and in
non-Roman terms as the community of believers:

> The Church, spread over the whole world even to the confines of
> the earth, has received from the Apostles and from their disciples
> faith in one God, the Father Almighty, who created heaven and
> earth and the sea and all that is in them; and in one Christ Jesus,
> the Son of God, who became incarnate for our salvation; and in
> the Holy Spirit, who by the prophets announced the dispositions
> and the comings and the virgin birth, the passion, the resurrection
> from the dead, and the ascension into heaven in the flesh, of the
> beloved Christ Jesus our Lord, and His coming from the heavens
> in the glory of the Father to recapitulate all things, and to raise up
> all human flesh, in order that to Christ Jesus our Lord and God and
> Saviour and King, every knee may bend, according to the good
> pleasure of the unseen Father.[11]

In *Demonstrations of the Apostolic Preaching*, Irenaeus argues
that by the Word of God (and by that Irenaeus always means the
acted-out nature, will, and power of God) everything is under
the sign of the economy of redemption, and the Son of God was

crucified for all and for everything precisely to restore the entire
human and material creation in himself. In this understanding the
whole of nature is associated with the destiny of man, for man
enfolds it and conditions its state. The central sentence reads:

> . . . it is the Word of God, the Son of God, Jesus Christ our Lord,
> who appeared to the prophets in the form described in their oracles
> and according to the special disposition of the Father; [the Word]
> by whom all things were made; and who, in the fullness of time,
> to recapitulate and contain all things, became man, in order to
> destroy death, to manifest life and to restore union between God
> and man.[12]

Perhaps because Irenaeus was a bishop, pastor, preacher, but
more certainly because the concreteness of his theological formulations were forged out of the vivid episodic speech of the Scriptures,
his writing has an earthy and dramatic character. Force impacts
against force, direction is violently reversed by a power turning it,
images clash in surprising juxtaposition. The Adam of the Garden
of Eden is recapitulated by the second Adam of the garden of
Gethsemane; a garden-rebellion is reenacted to redemption by a
garden-obedience. The first Eve who stood straight in autonomy is
recapitulated by the second—the bowed and rapt theonomous Eve
of the Magnificat. A summary sentence is:

> He recapitulated in Himself the long history of men, summing up
> and giving us salvation, in order that we might receive again in
> Christ Jesus what we had lost in Adam, that is, the image and
> likeness of God.[13]

Father Mersch, commenting upon the scope of the recapitulation
theme in Irenaeus, writes:

> He possesses most intimate relationships with all. Thus, accord-
> ing to a view that is peculiar to our Saint, Christ passed through all
> the ages of a man's life in order to sanctify them all in Himself;
> thus, too, the events of His mortal life have a perpetual influence
> upon our justification. In Him, we have all been obedient unto

death; in His Passion, we have all been roused from sleep, and when He ascended into heaven, we ascended with Him.

His work is one of solidarity and of unity. In dying, He traced the sign of the Cross upon all things, and, in the beautiful words uttered by one of the early Christians and recorded by Irenaeus, His two crucified arms, wide outstretched, were an appeal to union addressed to every nation.[14]

Professor Hugo Rahner chooses as his most summarizing paragraph from Irenaeus the following:

> The true Creator of the World is the Logos of God who is our Lord and who in these latter days became man. Although he is in the world, his power invisibly embraces all created things, and his mark has been set upon the whole of creation since he is the Word of God, who guides and orders all things. And that is why he came in visible form to that which was his own and became flesh and hung upon the wood, so that he might recapitulate the universe in himself.[15]

The "cosmic" Christology of Irenaeus cannot be dismissed by the too easy argument that its contours are determined by conflict with the gnostics. Specification of occasion does not dissolve consideration of substance. Other Fathers, their thought not shaped by gnostic claims, speak of God and Christ and grace and nature in the same organic way. The idea that the Incarnate Word is in himself the unity and harmony not only of men, but also of the entire material universe, was a theme that runs through virtually the whole of the writings of many influential Fathers. What differs in other treatments of the theme is the conceptualization of the notion of recapitulation, the particular language in which the image is expounded.

As the thought of the church came to center more and more upon the meaning of Incarnation rather than upon polemical defenses against gnosticism, the necessity to elaborate the force and scope of Incarnation determines ideas, language, and use of scripture. When, for instance, between 318 and 320 St. Athanasius was writing his tracts *Against the Pagans* and *On the Incarnation*, the occasion for the elaboration of a cosmic Christology is clearly not the gnostic heresy. Philosophical atomism seems to be the position against which Athanasius directs his words:

> The Greek philosophers say that the world is a great body. And in this they are right. For we see that the world and its parts are sensible things. If, then, the word of God resides in this world which is a body; if He is present in each and every thing, is there anything strange or absurd in our claim that the Word is present in man?
>
> Like a musician who has attuned his lyre, and by the artistic blending of low and high and medium tones produces a single melody, so the Wisdom of God, holding the universe like a lyre, adapting things heavenly to things earthly, and earthly things to heavenly, harmonizes them all, and, leading them by His will, makes one world and one world order in beauty and harmony.[16]

In that citation our point is clearly made. Irenaeus was confronting a cosmic demonology or angelology, and he threw against it a cosmic Christology. Athanasius was confronting in Arianism a cosmic religious psychology, and he threw against it an equally cosmic Christology of the divinization of all things in and by grace.

Grace, for Athanasius, was both a comprehensive term for the created goodness of all reality, and a term wherewith to specify the incarnated presence and historical focus of that Light which is God. The following paragraph by Jaroslav Pelikan is summary:

> One of the most persistent themes of Athanasian apologetics was this defense of the intrinsic goodness of reality against its detractors. And a frequent image for this defense was the metaphor of the light. If one accepted the proposition that the Logos of God was present throughout the universe, one would likewise have to grant that the entire universe was both illumined and moved by the Logos, from whom there came the light and movement and life of all things. Again, it was the Logos that granted light and life to the universe; and because the Logos had illumined all things, visible and invisible, it was the holy Logos of the Father that held

them all together. This goodness of all reality was built into the very structure of being by the Logos, who was the principle of life, light, and movement. Committed as he was to the defense of the salvation wrought by Christ, Athanasius did not, like Tertullian and some later theologians, find it necessary to denigrate nature in order to glorify grace. On the contrary, he took his stand as the defender of the goodness of nature against its detractors; for this defense of the goodness in all of reality was at the same time an act of praise for the God of grace. There was not only revelation in the creation; there was even grace in the creation.[17]

The words in the title of this chapter, "Some Crucial Moments," suggest the limits of it. No effort will be made to discuss the persistence of the theme of the relation of Christ and nature in patristic theology as a whole. For such a task I have not the competence, and the task has been performed in works that are easily available.[18] The intention is to say only enough to invite the reader to suspect that Christian tradition about this theme is richer, fuller, more broadly attested than is indicated in the manuals for history of doctrine most commonly used in the schools.

### The West—The Light That Lightens Every Man

So we turn now to another and later "moment" and choose St. Augustine, for two reasons. First, in his understanding of the grace of God in and with the creation, Augustine stands with catholic tradition; indeed he deepens and expands this tradition by the exquisite and probing analysis whereby he locates the operation of grace within the "natural" dynamics of man's loves, man's search for knowledge, and the solidification of man's will. But, second, aspects of Augustine's thought which, disengaged from his total theology, have been most influential in later doctrines of grace as popularly declared have worked to reduce that fuller understanding of grace to which he so richly contributed, and which is in continuity with the thought and spirit of Irenaeus.

How did so strange an outcome occur?

Students of intellectual history have often remarked how ideas of great generality and force may by circumstances be reduced to a single aspect of their fullness, or utilized for arguments so dramatic that a total context is forgotten. Something very like that has happened in the instance of Augustine's teaching about God's grace. The large and luminous light of grace permeates his writings. But the particular heresy he was called to combat has, for many, become normative for an understanding and assessment of his more comprehensive teaching. The general light of grace as Augustine affirmed it has been reduced to a laser beam for cauterizing the Pelagian error.

It would be unfair, untrue, and irresponsible to affirm that a study of St. Augustine on the doctrine of grace would disclose him to have intended so narrow or purely topical a reduction. It is very clear, however, that almost exclusive attention to grace within the rubric of *sin* and grace has fated his teaching to have been understood in such a diminished way. In Western thought Augustine lives in preaching, in catechesis, in moral counsel, and in general theological instruction principally in the sin-grace problem. One can sense the malproportion of this outcome if he examines Augustine's writings upon the knowledge of God, particularly in the *Confessions*, and in the treatise on *The Holy Trinity*. In these texts the doctrine of grace has the same topical centrality, the same "energy," the same sovereignty as it enjoyed in the earlier period to which we have attended.

One has only to follow Augustine in his description of the absolute efficacy of grace in that interior drama of reintegration of the love of self to the love of God—in the course of which man's incurvature is bent back to its intention—to absolve Augustine of any *formal* diminution of the power of grace. Augustine declares that just as it is a light of grace that "lights every man who comes into the world," so it is this same grace that abides with man and saves him from intellectual despair. The desire to know (*curiositas*), the study and systematization of empirical fact enables men to rise above the animal creation and become constructively human by relating means to ends in an ordered scheme of life. But this "good" of science is limited; it fails to disclose an end other than that of mere adjustment. Indeed, in the natural sciences, these "adjustments" have become enormous and range far beyond the dreams of Augustine. But their inability to satisfy the appetite for felicity is not only not reduced by the magnitude of such achievements, it is made thereby the more sardonic and bitter.

This view of *sapientia* or Christian wisdom as a basis for the judgment of value marks a final revolt from the spirit and method of Platonic science. Verbally, Augustinian *sapientia* is the exact equivalent of Plotinian NOŪS. For Plotinus, however, the function of NOŪS was to communicate with the One which is beyond knowledge and beyond being, and which is thus revealed—only in ecstacy. Augustinian *sapientia*, on the other hand, is emphatically not ecstatic and it presupposes no such detachment from the material world. As the judgment of value it is, indeed, "independent" of science and of the scientific discipline. That independence, however, serves merely to establish its right to supplement the deficiencies of science, by providing a fresh version of the cosmos and of man's place in it. In the light of *sapientia*, man no longer sees himself over against a "nature" conceived anthropomorphically whether as "thought" or "mechanism." On the contrary, he *sees himself and his universe together* (underlining mine) as an expression of beneficent activity, the activity of the creative and moving principle—in the language of religion, as a "creature" whose origin, nature, and destiny are determined by the will of God.[19]

Augustine was a bishop. He was responsible for instruction and guidance. In the exercise of that responsibility he could not always honor symmetry of presentation above the precision and force required by the moment's need. And the need of the moment in his century was to address the gospel of grace to two issues. The one was political, the other moral.

The political problem was to present to his age—in which the old power of the idea of the empire, now waning, was no longer

able to give unity and motive to men's energies—a total vision of
the origin, meaning, and destiny of political communities. The
image of the city of God was alone large enough and deep enough
to accomplish that.

Professor C. N. Cochrane gives a broad, superbly articulated,
and theologically sophisticated account of this achievement,[20] and
brings together the Christian faith and the moral and political
threat to the life of antiquity.

The moral problem was to clarify and propose a love adequate
to the imperious loves of men—a love with which we are beloved,
which should expose the futility of all lesser loves, relate them to
itself, and redeem their egocentric curvative into that adoration
which is both right will and true knowledge.

In this concentration of his thought upon grace for political
reconstruction of the community of men, and upon grace for the
moral renovation of the perverted will and the futile loves of men,
Augustine does not use the language of that cosmic Christology
which had been so clearly utilized in the tradition before his time.
The substance is there, however, and one has only to recall the
fullness of his meditation upon that "light that lighteth every man
that cometh into the world" and the "light which not only falls
upon things but is also within the eyes with which things are
beheld" to know this. Augustine's task was to speak to a historical
crisis and to a moral lostness. For that reason the relation of grace
to the world-as-nature does not receive from him an explicit discussion. But Augustine's teaching about the formation of the possibilities of knowledge in relation to the transegocentric love of God
by which man's loves are elevated, and the formation of a new
will in this process, clearly operates with an understanding of grace
which is continuous with the earlier tradition.

All of the preceding is by no means a pedantic fussing around
with ancient doctrines of grace. The effort is rather to locate and
administer, in continuity with the church's faith and in ways useful for our time, the reality of a gracious God. That reality is

always a disclosure creative of a response, and the point or theatre of its effective impact changes with man's self- and world-understanding. In a following chapter the implications of this fact will be dealt with. A concluding concern of this chapter is to point to aspects of contemporary theological reflection that attest how radically man's new situation in relation to the world-as-nature is determining his response-capacity to traditional proposals of the grace of God.

## The Dis-graced World

In the West two large patterns, descriptive of how grace and man's nature are related, have controlled Christian thought: a pattern based upon the analogy of being, and a pattern drawn from the primal divine activity of the Word of God. The first presupposes interior relations of possibility that the second does not necessarily suppose. But both are deeply in trouble. The analogy of being, in its older forms, draws checks on a metaphysical account that is exhausted; the second draws checks on an account that, while not exhausted, is presently undergoing such hermeneutical accounting that the checks are held up because of radical unclarity about what funds are really there.

In the meantime a new and earthy mode of analogy is emerging, and in its emergence is providing a different context and substance for all statements about the grace of God and man's response and possibility. Books bearing such titles as *Process and Reality, Faith and Culture, Christ and Cosmos, Redemption and Revolution, Ecological Man,* etc., suggest the natural context for fresh articulations of the Christian faith: it is an analogy rich in data drawn from man's embeddedness in nature, and assumes the truth of man's evolutionary identity as empirical fact. The creation, the Incarnation, and the natural world as place of grace—within that triangulation is the only present possibility for an intelligible grammar of grace and a rhetoric able to give it praise.

To the "crucial moments" already alluded to, several soundings into the sea of contemporary reflection about this issue may prove enlightening.

What characterizes very many modern efforts at christological reformulation is the direct, sometimes passionate probing for a Christ-understanding that shall speak to men within the grip of a twofold threat: (a) a disintegration of personhood so profound that the very realities of bond, covenant, respect, justice, and human preciousness are themselves no longer available for help, and, (b) an absurd, earth-destroying, life-mutilating, future-cancelling, and brutal attack upon the resources and life-supporting materials and processes of man's ancient place, the earth itself.

When he was Vicar of Great St. Mary's parish in Cambridge, Dean Hugh Montefiore declared that we need to redefine creatively the Chalcedonian terms of "nature" and "person." The paradox of grace is proposed as the best analogy by which the relation of the human and the divine in Jesus can be understood today.[21] The ancient notions of "nature" will no longer serve; and ancient ways of speaking about God's grace in Jesus Christ must attend to this fact. Montefiore's simplest statement is, "Jesus revealed the fullness of divine activity in human personality. In Jesus Christ the pattern of divine activity was revealed in a single historical life of a fully human person."[22] What is significant about the statement is not its substance (D. M. Baille had earlier said much the same), but that it should have been forged out of the two central concerns of the essay in which it appears—the crisis of love and regard among persons, and man's growing insensitivity to and positive abuse of the good earth. The realm of the "divine activity" (cf. Gregory Palamas's "energies" of Christ) is identical with all loves and perversions and operations of man's engaged life with the world beyond the self; its center is "you are accepted in grace"; its range and imperative is the gracious ethicizing of all the operations of the self.

Rosemary Reuther argues that that too narrow understanding of Augustine of which we have spoken, has indeed had fateful consequences:

. . . Augustine's stress on man's depravity tipped the balance of the Eastern view in the direction of an identification of man with his depravity. This disrupted the sense of man's continuing grounding in the grace of the original creation. The underlying continuity between the original creation and God's saving grace was disrupted, and grace became discontinuous and antithetical to nature. Man mounted up to God by cutting his ties with what was below and behind him. The ultimate direction of this concept of man could only end in a final rejection of that view of nature in which nature was seen as the gracious icon of God's face; and it could only result in a substitute view which made nature an enemy to be ruthlessly put under man's feet![23]

During the writing of this chapter Professor John Black published his *The Dominion of Man*,[24] a superb historical account of the grace-nature issue in Western thought and practice. The entire book is a parallel, but much more detailed and fully documented, account of the same shift to which Rosemary Reuther's article is addressed.[25]

One gathers material for theological reflection wherever he can find it, and much can come from places one is not looking for or at. Additional data for insight into that expansion of the realm of grace, and the longing to find the total meaning its bestowal promises, can be derived from the words and works of the artistic community.

For several years I was chairman of a commission representing many churches and assigned to inquire why it is that American artists are, for the most part, alienated from the terms, concepts, episodes, and symbols that set forth the Christian story. That they are so disengaged is both indubitable and strange. For this story, in its own terms and in its creativity within Western culture, has for many centuries been steady material for the exercise of the artistic vision, and for the translation of such vision into palpable forms. No generation before the present one would have thought of creating a commission on religion and the arts. Indeed, to have done so would have been regarded as a humorless bureaucratization of the obvious, like having a committee to study the relation of water and fish!

Our commission expected the artists to express alienation. We did not expect that the causes for such alienation would be so clearly and forcibly expressed, nor did we anticipate that such expressions would disclose so quickly and clearly the untheologically stated theological focus of the problem. The artist, painter, printmaker, dancer, actor, sculptor, novelist, poet, and musician is most commonly not only indifferent to the Christian story and without expectation that it has anything to say to him as an artist, he is angry about the churchly transmitters of that story.

Long exposure to the statements, eloquent nonstatements, disgusts, gestured feelings of the artist, and reflection upon these, has disclosed what I think is the heart of the matter. The artist carries on a lover's quarrel with the world; he is fascinated by the vivacity, variety, conflicts, delights, and torments of life, and he is maddened into creativity by the endless effort to give this reality "a local habitation and a name." He sees his work as the patient and alert evocation of a secret. He is the midwife of the elusive, the siren of the timid, the articulator of the silent, the telltale of forms of life en route to becoming.

The artist loves the palpable and the immediate, the forms, shapes, colors, textures, movements, and the mad or recurring intersections of life. It is this very recalcitrance of the given actualities before his attack which is both his allure and his problem. And, rightly or wrongly, he feels that this living stuff of natural life is either indifferently regarded or negatively assessed by the community which is Christ's church. Or, if it is not rejected, both it and the artist are *used*, which is, in his judgment, a mere commodity-evaluation and utilization of the stuff of his dedication. The church, says the artist, thinks itself spiritually above the gross materialities of the artist's shop, or theatre, or lonely place of struggle. But it has nevertheless managed, despite this transmaterial spirituality, to have got on very well in this world. The church seems to him unmoved by the artist's effort to bring to the surface those inchoate allurements of unity and significance, those secrets eloquent of our common human reality, which constitute both the pathos and the glory of mankind. The "spirituality" of the church appears to the artist as an abstraction when affirmed apart from the "spirituality" enfolded in things and persons and natural vitalities. He has an understandable feeling that all exposure of the real serves the truth; and if the truth of the Christian faith be indeed not *identical* with artistic truth, no "higher order" of truth ought despise the actual. It is precisely this negative assessment which the artist gathers from what I have called the "use" of the labor of the artist. The church "hires" the artist to paint, design, or write, but with the superior assumption that the bundle of palpable immediacies with which the artist works must serve a higher order of truth before their own truth and integrity can be accredited.

The artist who has

> . . . heard inside each mortal thing
> Its holy emanation sing[26]

is not a preacher of the gospel of the divine grace; it is quite possible that he may be the tongue to that living voice and form of "common grace" which, in terrible knowledge of what will *not* suffice, "goes before the face of the Lord to prepare his way." For if, as the letter to the Ephesians asserts, "in the futility of our minds . . . we are darkened in understanding," "alienated from God because of ignorance produced by callousness and hardness of heart" (Eph. 4:17–18), then all that serves to lighten darkness, inform ignorance, sensitize callousness, and pierce hardness serves grace—without the name or intention so to do.

# 4.

# Grace in Post-Reformation Culture

The purpose of this chapter is so to lead the reader from the biblical and early church reflections about God's grace and through the intervening centuries as to set him before the meaning and the problems of grace as that meaning, or lack of it, confronts the mind and sensibility of our time.

The foregoing discussion makes it now possible to attempt such a general statement about grace as shall sum up biblical and early Christian thought: grace is an action and gift of God whereby there is made possible a relationship to God that is otherwise impossible; what man *is* and becomes by the grace of God is not identical with what he could become simply in virtue of his existence as a human being. Catholic theology has often regarded creation itself as a gracious gift; the redemption of man within sustained existence is a further gift of grace. Man lives, that is to say, as a creature of a "double gratuity."

This understanding of grace as a gift of a new God-relationship has been variously understood in the several theological traditions, but central to all of them are three points which have been succinctly specified by Professor Eugene TeSelle:

As its origin, grace is the favor of God toward men, a free decision of love in their behalf. Grace is also the communication of this divine decision to men, whether the emphasis falls upon historical events (as in much of modern theology), or upon human words whose content is heard as revelation and thus becomes the power of God for salvation (as in classical Protestantism), or upon men (as is usual in Catholic theology). Whatever the means may be, the original divine decision is effectively communicated to man. Considered at its goal, grace is viewed as the intended aim of the divine decision and its communication to man.[1]

That paragraph about the origin, communication, and goal of grace, while clear and responsible, nevertheless puts the reader promptly before the problem of all theological speech about grace. For the terms "origin," "communication," and "goal" are not static-substantial but dynamic-historical terms. Grace is indeed commonly postulated as the elemental character of God in his relation to all that is not God. That postulation roots the reality of grace, not in some ontology of God, but in the confessed witness to God as he is understood through men's interpretation of historical and experiential encounters. Grace not only communicates a God so understood; grace is that God-as-communicating nothing less or other than himself as Presence. And the goal of grace is not accurately designated by the old phrase "state of grace." It is better put when the relational and continuing character of the work, goal, end, purpose, and gift of grace is understood as creative of a new relationship of all things to God, who gives himself in grace, new relationship to the fellowman (who is the fellow creature bound to God in a covenant of grace), new relationship to the nonhuman creation within which grace also resides and because it, too, is God's creation.[2] How grace, thus understood, addresses contemporary man will be the effort of the essays to follow this chapter. Three intermediate and preparatory topics require discussion at this point.

## Reformation Precision about Grace

If one were to have in mind the complex of forces that constituted the Reformation of the sixteenth century, and were to make an effort to pierce through the ecclesiological, doctrinal, political, social, economic, and personal data in order to specify the fundamental affirmation enunciated by those convulsive decades, one could defend this general statement: the Reformation was a vehement witness to the freedom of God in his grace.[3] A second statement could be defended as true of what followed upon the truth and vehemence of that central affirmation: that the precision of the reformers and the Reformation-born confessions about grace restricted the scope of that very grace which they so faithfully specified as central to Christian faith and life.

How did this diminishment of the scope of grace come about?

Throughout the whole of Western Christendom, from a time at least as early as Augustine, the reality of grace had been explored and explicated within the rubric of *sin* and grace. When the reformers and, following them, virtually all of classical Protestant theology spoke of the grace of God they meant

> . . . the free and unmerited disposition and activity of God for the benefit of the sinner, overcoming his bondage to sin (in Luther, sin, the law, death, and the devil), restoring him to the life for which he was originally intended.[4]

There were reasons for this intense concentration of the meaning of grace at the point of sin. Among them, these: the reinforcement of the morally mordant strand of Christian teaching by the disorder, violence, economic misery, and disease-vulnerability that stalked the common life; the waning of a meaning-giving order in thought and feeling and sensibility in all aspects of common life as the medieval world of the West played out to the end the images, ideas, and institutions that had formed it for a thousand years; a slowly rising sense for the reality and authenticity of personal judgment, experience, and thought as the force of the immediately and experimentally known collided with an ever more formalized voice of a deepeningly politicized and bureaucratic church. The realities of grace were identified with and available only through a sacerdotalized clergy, a substantialized sacrament, and almost mathematized procedures for the achievement of redemption.[5]

The reality of the freedom of God in his grace is at once the charter of the church, the treasure of the church, and the interior corrective to all triumphalism, both doctrinal and institutional. Where sin is the heart of the problem the gospel of the freedom of God in his grace toward sinners is the answer. That sin was the heart of the problem in the fifteenth and sixteenth centuries, and that the proclamation of the primacy of grace was the effective answer is attested by that time's popular moral theology, books of meditation, religious, secular, and popular art, hymnody, morality plays, and legends. Therefore, the absolute concentration of the reality of grace at the point of Christ as that action of God in whom sinners are forgiven *sola gratia*. *Sola gratia* was not only a true but a tactically necessary focus for the doctrine in that time and situation. For the *sola* spoke both of the source of grace and of the place of its encounter.

Whether that precision and absolute accent is equally appropriate for another time and a quite different situation is a separate problem to which we shall return in a later section.

## Enlightenment Displacement of Grace

Back of the Enlightenment, and necessary to an understanding of its amazing redirection of Western man's thought and action, stands that equally amazing and vivacious phenomenon called the Renaissance. The personalities, events, discoveries, and developments that are episodes of the Renaissance and suggest its scope and force are admirably summarized in a paragraph from John Addington Symonds. The modern reader will have undergone experiences that cause him to smile over the humanistic expansiveness of the passage. But the sardonic smile in the present is as educative for us as the sonorous confidence of the late nineteenth century essayist is reportorial of a cast of mind entirely representative of one powerful strand of nineteenth century confidence and expectation:

. . . we cannot refer the whole phenomena of the Renaissance to any one cause or circumstance, or limit them within the field of any one department of human knowledge. If we ask the students of art what they mean by the Renaissance, they will reply that it was the revolution effected in architecture, painting, and sculpture by the recovery of antique monuments. Students of literature, philosophy, and theology see in the Renaissance that discovery of manuscripts, that passion for antiquity, that progress in philology and criticism, which led to a correct knowledge of the classics, to a fresh taste in poetry, to new systems of thought, to more accurate analysis, and finally to the Lutheran schism and the emancipation of the conscience. Men of science will discourse about the discovery of the solar system by Copernicus and Galileo, the anatomy of Vesalius, and Harvey's theory of the circulation of the blood. The origination of a truly scientific method is the point which interests them most in the Renaissance. The political historian, again, has his own answer to the question. The extinction of feudalism, the development of the great nationalities of Europe, the growth of monarchy, the limitation of the ecclesiastical authority and the erection of the Papacy into an Italian kingdom, and in the last place the gradual emergence of that sense of popular freedom which exploded in the Revolution; these are the aspects of the movement which engross his attention. Jurists will describe the dissolution of legal fictions based upon the False Decretals, the acquisition of a true text of the Roman Code, and the attempt to introduce a rational method into the theory of modern jurisprudence, as well as to commence the study of international law. Men whose attention has been turned to the history of discoveries and inventions will relate the exploration of America and the East, or will point to the benefits conferred upon the world by the arts of printing and engraving, by the compass and the telescope, by paper and by gunpowder; and will insist that at the moment of the Renaissance all these instruments of mechanical utility started into existence, to aid the dissolution of what was rotten and must perish, to strengthen and perpetuate the new and useful and life-giving. Yet neither any one of these answers taken separately, nor indeed all of them together, will offer a solution of the problem. By the term Renaissance, or new birth, is indicated a natural movement, not to be explained by this or that characteristic, but to be accepted as an effort of humanity for which at length the time had come, and in the onward progress of which we still participate. The history of the Renaissance is not the history of arts, or of sciences, or of literature, or even of nations. It is the history of the attainment of self-conscious freedom by the human spirit manifested in the European races. It is no mere political mutation, no new fashion of art, no restoration of classical standards of taste. The arts and the inventions, the knowledge and the books, which suddenly became vital at the time of the Renaissance, had long lain neglected on the shores of the Dead Sea which we call the Middle Ages. It was not their discovery which caused the Renaissance. But it was the intellectual energy, the spontanaeous outburst of intelligence, which enabled mankind at that moment to make use of them. The force then generated still continues, vital and expansive, in the spirit of the modern world.[6]

The energies, goals, and accomplishments so amply detailed in this passage were, in the period of Enlightenment that followed, organized by empirical reason. Men resolved to make themselves fully at home in the world of time and space. In the passion of that resolution there developed a way of thinking and feeling that gave birth to all that is characteristic of modernity. The opening sentence of the essay "Enlightenment" in the Encyclopaedia Britannica reads:

. . . a movement of thought and belief, developed from interrelated conceptions of God, reason, nature and man, to which there was wide assent in Europe during the 17th and 18th centuries. Its dominant conviction was that right reasoning could find true knowledge and could lead mankind to felicity.

The intention of the term "displacement" as the designation of this section can be made instantly clear by setting over against that encyclopedia statement some memorable words from the liturgical prayers of the church during the seventeen hundred years that preceded the period of Enlightenment. What did common men and women in a hundred thousand village parishes and cathedrals understand, assess, and mean when they spoke of the grace of God? Whence and by whose gift was that power and presence in which men trusted to ". . . lead mankind to felicity"? The lan-

guage of these prayers is, indeed, often an Elizabethan English
translation of Latin Collects; but as that *cantus firmus* sings on
beneath the changes of formal theology, no one with any sense for
the stubborn continuity of devotion can miss in these words the
catholic substance of faith.

> O God, the strength of all them that put their trust in thee: Merci-
> fully accept our prayers; and because through the weakness of our
> mortal nature we can do no good thing without thee, grant us the
> help of thy grace . . .
> > (Collect for First Sunday after Trinity).
> Lord, we pray thee, that thy grace may always go before and follow
> after us, and make us continually to be given to all good works . . .
> > (Collect for Sixteenth Sunday after Trinity).

That the grace of God, preceding, attending, judging, consoling,
enfolding, was the elemental context of the ever so ambiguous
Christian culture of the West marks also the Prayer for the Dead.
In this prayer grace is the guarantor and content of that felicity
which, in Enlightenment culture, was differently located.

> Almighty God, with whom do live the spirits of those who depart
> hence in the Lord—and with whom the souls of the faithful, after
> they are delivered from the burden of the flesh, are in joy and
> felicity: We give thee hearty thanks for thy grace bestowed upon
> thy servants, who, having finished their course in faith, do now rest
> from their labors. . . .

The point is clear. The fundamental conviction of Enlightenment
culture was that ultimate human felicity was attainable and was
to be sought in the strength of rational thought and action. The
grace of God was acknowledged, celebrated, and even called upon,
but the effectual reality of it was displaced from the center of the
human story, and gradually replaced by another confidence, another
possibility for fulfillment, and another center of hope. It is not
necessary to detail here the steps of that process or cite the spokes-
men for it. Our present purpose is but to recognize and assess the
theological requirements placed upon us by the outcome.[7]

## Contemporary Man and the Relocation of Grace

Under this topic, looking back to the mainly biblical and historical substance of the foregoing discussion and looking ahead to a concrete description of the context of life today, it is both possible and necessary to sketch out the fundamental lines of an expanded Christian doctrine of grace. To have attempted that earlier would have left the argument arbitrary and hanging in midair; to defer the effort longer would leave the following pages without an interpretive focus for the reader.

Two observations must precede the effort. The first observation is notice served upon those who stand theologically to my left that I find the juicy vocabulary of joy, celebration, dancing, and feasting, to be an engaging but rootless body of admonition unless the ancient, steady reality of the *hilaritas* of a gracious God is its ground and its exhaustless energy. The second observation is notice to those who stand theologically to my right that when, in the sections to follow, I reflect about grace "beyond" the language, concepts, images, propositions, and contexts of the Scripture, that reflection is a product of the Scripture whose modes I find it faithful to transcend. Such reflection "beyond" Scripture does not mean that the what, and the from-where, and the energy-born witness to grace is "beyond" what Scripture affirms; it does mean that how, in the Bible, men grasped by the reality of God beheld and understood and dealt with themselves, their fellowmen, and the world is a fact that must be stated "beyond" the biblical mode if God and grace and contemporary men and their world are to be served.[8]

### 1) The Meaning of Grace

All Christian theology appeals to the reality of grace to specify its central intention when it speaks of God. This is as true of Christian philosophical theology as it is true of biblical, dogmatic, and moral theology. The God of A. N. Whitehead is as fundamentally a gracious God as the God of Karl Barth. To speak of God as gracious is to say that what we mean by God is a creative and redeeming reality, presence, energy, and allure, and that all manifestation of this reality, whether clear or masked, unequivocal or ambiguous, so ultimately discloses God—not fully to knowledge, but sufficiently to acknowledgment in faith—that the reality of God as loving, sustaining, and fulfilling power for the life of the world is the central confession of the community of faith. One of the forces that inwardly demanded the formulation of Trinitarian confessions about God was clearly the necessity to ground the enpersonalized, incarnated, and historical incandescence of grace in Jesus Christ absolutely within the reality of God. "Grace . . . came by Jesus Christ," but grace was not created by Jesus Christ. The substantive, *grace,* functions historically in the verb *came.* God, who is gracious, once took this way of actualizing his grace. And the Spirit who "leads into truth" is the functioning of the reality of grace in time-occasioned, but not time-bound, and ever-fresh ways.

Grace is the fundamental ascription that Christian faith must make in the God-relationship. It is that particular "attribute" or reality, or energy, essence, or substance of the God of Abraham, Isaac, and Jacob, and of Jesus Christ; and every theological method that would seek to be reflectively and reflexively adequate to the faith of the community founded by faith in this God must probe and grope for concepts to designate and a language to distinguish and celebrate this particularity. The church's experience of and reflection upon the reality of grace could not stop short of a doctrine of the Trinity for the reason that what that experience disclosed could not be confined to Jesus in his individuality, or to the spirit as ". . . the Lord and Giver of Life, Who proceedeth from the Father and the Son, . . . Who spoke by the Prophets." All is of grace, and the One God is a God of grace.

This recollection of the Trinitarian amplitude of the church's explication of the meaning of grace suggests what must be the scope and effective arena of grace.

## 2) The Place of Grace

The reality of grace defines the place of grace. If grace is postulated of God the Creator, God the Redeemer, and God the Sanctifier, then the presence and power and availability of grace must be postulated with equivalent scope. There has never been a time in the church's history when this requirement has been formally denied; there have been times when the point has been effectually forgotten, or when situations arose that tempted to such exclusive accent upon the christological or the Spirit-focus that grace and the creation were suppressed into practical denial.

It is exactly the point of the foregoing paragraphs to suggest that the entire life-experience of post-Enlightenment man demands the recovery of catholic comprehensiveness in the doctrine of grace. The assertion that the reality of grace must be "relocated" in the spheres of creation where contemporary man's operational actuality is most clearly evidenced, and amidst those tormented movings of the Spirit toward a transtechnical realization of men's common humanity in personhood fulfilled in justice, peace, and mutual recognition, is not a "relocation" that proposes a novelty; it is, rather, an appeal for the restitution of an almost forgotten dimension.[9]

This relocation of grace within the actuality of man's life within history and nature, and amidst the most common and formative episodes of experience, is not only a formal requirement of the interior energy of the plentitude of grace itself; it is an absolute requirement arising from the post-Enlightenment embeddedness of man's mind, self-assessment, and operational life in the world. If, therefore, the proposal of grace is not made to man in the matrix of his life-situation, the proposal is either unintelligible or uninteresting.

This "embeddedness" has generated enormous reportorial attention; the literature descriptive of the secular man, and the responses of the religious community to the process of secularization is abundant. But it is necessary for theological analysis to go

beyond both such tracings of historical causation and of sociological description of behavioral changes. Theology must ask:
What has happened within the mind of modernity that changes
how that mind and sensibility *hears* the term "grace"?

When our fathers heard the word grace, they *heard* it from
within a thought- and world-structure that had existed fundamentally unchanged for centuries. Grace, originating in the will of
God, concretized in a historical appearance, was a sovereign holy
resource for the overcoming of man's sinful alienation from God,
a therapy for souls in the custody of the church. The very term
"the means of Grace" confirmed the notion of grace as a gift and
a power from God given to men.

That word of grace, in that mode of proposal, is no longer either
clear or persuasive. The entire hearing-situation has changed
because of the complete shattering of the anthropology presupposed
in it. The place for the encounter with grace has to be relocated
within that self- and world-knowledge and understanding which
is the huge and accumulating story of Western culture from Galileo
to the present. The possibilities-of-intelligibility are given by and
within the powerful presupposition about self, world, and their
relations. *That* is what has changed. Terms which for hundreds of
years presupposed our model of world-origin, -structure, and
-process, and were thus a matrix within which a language could
be shaped to articulate both man's need and God's grace, have
been either annihilated or have gone silently out of mind.

An illustration of this cultural emptying of language and the
refilling of the evacuated space by new fundamental notions can
be gained by attention to a statement from Alfred North Whitehead. The statement gains force by remembering that it predates
the recondite mathematical and physical sciences research by which
its speculative vision was later substantiated. What Whitehead
was saying softly and to the very few who had the knowledge to
understand him in 1933 is now a commonplace in high school
classes in general science.

The philosopher is speaking of the changed meaning of the word "location." He writes:

> Modern physics has abandoned the doctrine of Simple Location. The physical things which we term stars, planets, lumps of matter, molecules, electrons, protons, quanta of energy are each to be conceived as modifications of conditions within space-time, extending throughout its whole range. There is a focal region, which in common speech is where the thing is. But its influence streams away from it with finite velocity throughout the utmost recesses of space and time. . . . For physics, the thing itself is what it does, and what it does is this divergent stream of influence. Again the focal region cannot be conceived as an instantaneous fact. It is a state of agitation and differing from the so-called external stream by its superior dominance within the focal region. Also we are puzzled how to express exactly the existence of these physical things at any definite moment of time. For at every instantaneous point-event within or without the focal region, the modification to be ascribed to this thing is antecedent to, or successive to, the corresponding modification introduced by that thing at another point-event. Thus if we endeavor to conceive a complete instance of the existence of the physical thing in question, we cannot confine ourselves to one part of space or one moment of time.[10]

In such language is communicated that radical shift of world-understanding which has created the difficulty of "hearing" the old language of the old tradition when its affirmations are made in the old way. What things and forces and realities might be, how they operate, where they must be specified at work if they are to be conceived at all—these are proposals for reflection that are dead upon utterance if they fail to intersect with the mind's primal cognitive vocabulary. That vocabulary may be most generally designated as a vocabulary of reality-in-relations. Things are what they are, and do what they do, and have the force they have because they are *where* they are in a vast and intricate ecosystem. Just as the "where" of a thing demands systems-models for its adequate explication, so the nature and force and the promise of an energy (like grace) cannot even be proposed-for-faith if the proposal stumbles over discarded concepts.

Grace is not nature and nature is not grace. But grace and nature are related. No description of that relationship can of itself impart grace, but an unintelligible proposal can impede the mind's hearing of what is proposed for faith. The "relocation" of the reality of grace within the Trinitarian plentitude of God-proposal is here advocated because the God of grace *is* a God of grace in the fullness of his being as Creator, Redeemer, and Sanctifier. Such a relocation is not a diminution; it is rather a restoration of the place of encounter to the amplitude of the life-theatre in which man actually lives, experiences, thinks, wonders, and works. The "grace of the Lord Jesus Christ" is like the ". . . focal region which, in common speech, is where a thing is." The region of grace is all that is, has been, and will be; that is exactly what is meant by the New Testament ascription of Alpha and Omega, ". . . the first and the last, the beginning and the end." When, in the concluding verse of the eleventh chapter of Romans, the "gracious gifts of God" (verse 29) are recalled as of such scope and power to evoke the total response to total mercy in the paragraph beginning "O depth of wealth, wisdom, and knowledge in God," the occasion and focal point of this mercy is indeed the gospel of Christ. But the focal region of God's grace is not less than the whole creation. "Source, Guide, and Goal for all that is—to him be glory for ever. Amen" (NEB).[11]

## 3) The Occasions of Grace

If "the freedom of God in his grace" is a right designation of the central substance of the Christian confession, then any systematization of the modes, operations, intersections, and redemptive powers of that grace within man's historical existence must be appropriately modest. If, to put the matter another way, we postulate freedom of God in his disposition of grace, we must reciprocally postulate an open, incalculable, nonpredictive structure for man's encounter with and joy in it.[12] This is only to say that in theology, as in other realms of discourse, the systematization of freedom is a perilous undertaking.

Such an understanding grounds the choice of the term "occasions" for this section. For the term suggests and recalls the lively unexpectedness of the bestowals of grace in the Gospels: "And suddenly," ". . . and on the way he met . . . ," ". . . now it happened that . . . ," ". . . there stood before him a man. . . ." In the midst of the many-threaded, wild unsystematic of the actual, the not-expected was crossed and blessed by the not-possible.[13]

Such an understanding of the surprise, the might-not-have-been, the indeterminable quality of God's grace, so episodically rich in the Gospels, has been made difficult of recovery by a theological tradition that has made of grace a "datum" or a "state" or a steady and stable "quality" or "attribute" of God. If, on the contrary, grace is understood as the energy of love, having its origin in the freedom of God who finds "occasions" for the bestowal of that love, not in the regularities of *law*, but in and by the instant and uncalculated response to man in the matrix of the historical madness of human cussedness and glory, that is, according to the dynamics of *gospel*, then the "occasion" of grace must be thought of in fresh ways. The common life is the "happening-place" of it, and man as man in nature and in history supplies its normal occasions.

There is an absolute distinction between the cause of grace and the occasions of grace. Destruction from a gas explosion is not caused by a spark; it is occasioned by it. Nothing natural is the cause of grace; anything natural (or historical) may be an occasion of it. The disclosure of grace in the enormous paradox of the cross is the "focal point" for man's encounter with grace. The grace of God is humanly, historically, and episodically incandescent in Calvary. That occasion, indeed, was and is so crucial an occasion that the mind and devotion of the devout is tempted to forget, in its grateful Christocentrism, that Jesus was not centered in Jesus at all. He is called the Christ precisely because of that. Our theology can be Christocentric as regards the reality and crucial occasion of grace precisely because that Christology lives within the grace of the Holy Trinity. The holy occasion of the discovery of the grace of God may indeed be the mountaintop experience, but the place and content of the experience is not identical with the experienced in its origin and fullness and destiny. That is why the occasion must be both absolutely valued and absolutely qualified. For the decisive context of life is time as continuity and not time as moment; continuity, not break; steadiness, not staccato; what goes on and not only what shakes up.

All of this is but a way of saying that the reality of grace is the fundamental reality of God the Creator in his creation, God the Redeemer in his redemption, and God the Sanctifier and Illuminator in all occasions of the common life where sanctifying grace is beheld, bestowed, and lived by.

Is it possible to lay aside for the moment the quite proper Christian acknowledgment of grace as primarily an overcoming of alienation from God by God's action of forgiveness, and ask what is grace as a sheer phenomenon? That is both possible and necessary. When we do that, we see that what we mean by the term, pretheologically and conceptually, is grace as the sheer *givenness-character* of life, the world, and the self—the plain *presentedness* of all that is. The underside of this sheer gratuity, the givenness quality of things, supplies the subjective vocabulary by which that unaccountability is recognized; it is surprise, wonder, Tillich's "ontological shock." The term "gratuity of grace" includes both the knowledge of the gift and the astonishment that all that is is "gifted."[14]

This appeal to the phenomenonological core of grace-as-such, and an effort to specify that core as "sheer givenness" is not to be easily dismissed as an instance of pantheism, panentheism, or, in general, a theological procedure tinctured by poetic sensibility. The appeal proceeds rather from a hardheaded Trinitarian assumption that, as St. Thomas says, "God is above all things by the excellence of his nature; nevertheless he is in all things as causing the being of all things." It does not follow that man can move from nature to grace. It does follow with immutable force that he must move from the focal point of the incarnated embodiment and disclosure of grace to the creation as a theatre of grace. The Christian doctrine of redemption stands alongside the Christian doctrine of creation. Both doctrines postulate meaning; both specify that meaning in relation to the doctrine of God. The reality of God is working itself out, as it were, in both realms—the world-as-nature and the world-as-history. And these two "mighty workings" must be related. If there is postulated a logos-toward-redemption at work in history, and if the Lord who is disclosed there is postulated as the Lord of all that is, then this same comprehensiveness must inhere in an adequate Christology. Indeed, the earliest Christian communities, as we saw in an earlier chapter, felt the force of this momentum in their ascriptive doxologies to Christ and expressed it. Nature, that is to say, is an "occasioning" context, an interlaced web of origin and sustenance without which man is not. Where, in the eighth chapter of Romans, St. Paul sings his great song of redemption, he cannot halt the reality of it short of the creation itself—trapped indeed in futility, but waiting in longing and expectation.

This very notion of a primal "givenness" about all that is is a difficult one for a scientific and technological culture to apprehend. When analysis, classification, control, and management of fundamental components of natural life—atoms, cells, chromosomes, genes, etc.—has become ordinary, taken for granted, the blunt datum that all of this is sheerly "there" and "given" is an elemental fact that is muted or forgotten in and by virtue of the operations with it. What we do with the given is so astounding that the given-as-given becomes an unthought starting place for thought, a no longer surprising datum awaiting scientific transformations. The mind filled with the excitements of what men do with the components of the world works to blunt primitive astonishment before the fact that there is a world to do something with and men to do it.

Efforts of conceptual, systematic speech either to disclose this blunting of awareness or to correct it are futile. The hauteur of theologians toward the work of those who seek a language to give a "local habitation and a name" to that surprise-in-things which slips through the coarse net of generalizing language does nothing to help and much to hinder. To suppose that "occasions of grace" can be specified without a language that catches that bright and absolutely *particular* which shocks the mind into astonished awareness, and to that startled thankfulness for things that are, is to suppose the impossible.

Without apology, therefore, and in the conviction that theological repudiation of factic speech is a stupefaction that constitutes the problem rather than a sterile purity of intellection that might help toward a solution—and in the spirit of e. e. cummings's blazing ascription:

> i thank You God most for this amazing
> day: for the leaping greenly spirits of trees
> and a blue true dream of sky; and for everything
> which is natural which is infinite which is yes.[15]

I adduce the quieter evidence of another poet to the joy and gratitude that is evoked by the primal and the factic. The poem is called "Objects"; from the end of the third stanza it reads:

. . . Among the wedding gifts

> Of Herë, were a set
> Of golden McIntoshes, from the Greek
> Imagination. Guard and gild what's common, and forget
> Uses and prices and names; have objects speak.

> There's classic and there's quaint,
> And then there is that devout intransitive eye
> Of Pieter de Hooch: see feinting from his plot of paint
> The trench of light on boards, the much-mended dry

Courtyard wall of brick,
And sun submerged in beer, and streaming in glasses,
The weave of a sleeve, the careful and undulant tile. A quick
Change of the eye and all this calmly passes

Into a day, into magic.
For is there any end to true textures, to true
Integuments; do they ever desist from tacit, tragic
Fading away? Oh maculate, cracked, askew,

Gay-pocked and potsherd world
I voyage, where in every tangible tree
I see afloat among the leaves, all calm and curled,
The Cheshire smile which sets me fearfully free.[16]

# 5.

# Grace and a Sense for the World

It has been the latent but controlling supposition of the entire preceding discussion that intelligible proposals of the grace of God presently require a reconstitution of theological and religious language; that such a reconstitution must include both the language for specifying the faith which we believe as objective to the mind's beholding, and the faith whereby we believe as interior to the beholding mind. It is a further presupposition that such a reconstitution and relocation of language is not advanced by the multiplication of fervent pleas that it be done, or by a frantic recoloration of ancient terms in ever so psychedelic hues transferred from the paint box of merely contemporary sensibility.

The task is harder than that. Fundamental terms must be retraced to their multiple roots in the subsoil of a rich and varied tradition, their possibility for new life and force and clarity *as proposals* reassessed in terms of what ultimate pointings, structures, and possibilities of meaning inherent in them exude, bear forth, and freshly address contemporary knowledge, need, modes of cognition, and feeling-for-fact.

The "grace of God" is a term that demands such a procedure.

In the several sections of the present chapter we shall look at some of the components that make our time a literally new time in man's experience, and in such an excursion try to designate, in events of art, literature, and common experience, materials for reconstitution that lie at hand.

In the carrying out of that task a double-movement is required at every point: (a) the powers, intersections, and liberations of grace—because these were first witnessed to in episodes whose surprising nature both specified the reality and named it *grace*—must be honored by absolute attention to their historical particularity; (b) the holy and the human potential for the bestowing and the receiving of grace must not be limited to the various *mythoi* of its bestowal, acceptance, recognition, or of its accumulated fiducial burden in past acknowledgments.

The preceding chapter ended with a poem. The lines of the poem in themselves, and the use of those lines as a tactic for the advancement of the argument of these pages, are deliberate and intentional. For men do "guard and gild what's common." To inquire with the mind why they do that, and rejoice with delight and a lifting of the heart because they do that, is to place oneself at the center of what this chapter aspires to illuminate, a "sense for the world." We want to ask, for instance, what it means that Van Gogh so paints a pair of old shoes that there is evoked from the beholder a deep sense of both the terror and the dignity of man's common humanity, and a smiling sense of our fellowship with it; that Edward Hopper can so paint a figure enclosed in solitariness, sitting upon a stool in a garish, neon-brilliant corner of an all-night eating-joint starkly contrasted with the immense darkness of the midnight city, that the call of loneliness to loneliness is "guarded and gilded" in an iconography of recognition; that in all ages mighty works of literature ". . . traffic not with cold, celestial certainty, but with men's hopes and fears and breakings of the heart, all that gladdens, saddens, maddens us men and women in this brief and mutable traject . . ." of life in the creation which is our home for a while, the anchorage of our actual selves.[1]

The purpose of these paragraphs is not simply to state but to illustrate that nature and grace, perception, experience, and wonder, the creation as the habitat of our bodies, and the divine redemption as the Word of God to our spirits, must all be held together in thought as indeed they occur together in fact. And if, in the elaboration of this notion, the sober statement of the artist is adduced as useful, the absence of a theological label upon such evidence is of no significance. If, as has been noted, the occasions of grace, both in Israel's experience and in the testimony of the Christian community are incarnate—for Israel in her historical experience of liberation and God-heldness, for the Christian community in the "glory" of God beheld in "the face of Christ Jesus" —the place of grace must be the webbed connectedness of man's creaturely life. That web does not indeed bestow grace; it is necessarily the theatre for that anguish and delight, that maturation of longing and hope, that solidification of knowledge that can attain, as regards ultimate issues, not a clean, crisp certainty but rather the knowledge that:

> We who must die demand a miracle.
> How could the Eternal do a temporal act,
> The Infinite become a finite fact?
> Nothing can save us that is possible:
> We who must die demand a miracle.[2]

This turning to experience is not a way to account for grace; it may well be a prologomenon to the possibility of what Karl Rahner calls a "transcendental anthropology," by a way the artist affirms in his own concrete and earthy vision. Joseph Conrad, for instance:

> He [the artist] speaks to our capacity for delight and wonder, to the sense of mystery surrounding our lives; to our sense of pity, and beauty, and pain; to the latent feeling of fellowship with all creation—and to the subtle but invincible conviction of solidarity that knits together the loneliness of innumerable hearts, to the solidarity in dreams, in joy, in sorrow, in aspirations, in illusions, in hope, in fear, which binds men to each other, which binds together all humanity—the dead to the living and the living to the unborn.[3]

Or Henry James:

> Experience is never limited and it is never complete, it is an
> immense sensibility, a kind of huge spider-web of the finest silken
> threads suspended in the chamber of consciousness, and catching
> every air-borne particle in its tissue.[4]

## Grace and the Independence of the World-as-Nature

This section is interposed at this point because the issue of the
status of the universe must be rightly put if any proposals about
God, or grace, or "occasion" within human life and nature are
credibly open to the interpretations of faith. If the status of the
universe is assessed to be a "closed system" then we are called
upon to understand it without reference to anything outside it.[5]

But the universe is not closed to God's agency. The basic issue
of the universe itself has not been settled, and there seems to be
no possibility that it can be settled. Among many philosophers it
is said that we do not know whether the universe is the sort of
thing that has a reason for its existence. The question of its *status*
is an open question.

The enormous and growing body of knowledge about the structure and processes of the universe has caused contemporary theology to become silent about an issue that once preoccupied theologians. The "proofs" for the existence of God really were intended
to establish the dependence of the universe upon God. These
"proofs," ancient and modern, are in disarray; as a result, the
place and scope for any agency of God is restricted to the realms
of the historical, the social, and the solitary personal.

At the very moment such a contraction of the realm of meaning
is acquiesced to, one is aware that the scope of satisfactory meaning has been isolated from the massive context within which the
*question* of meaning arises, and apart from which its urgency
cannot be quieted. In a world known by cosmology, anthropology,
biology, and virtually every other basic discipline, the mind's

demand for proposals of "total meaning" is the matrix of the question.

It is, therefore, of high importance that, in the midst of ordered, growing, and verifiable knowledge about the structure and process of the universe we remain clear about the question theology asks, and must always ask. Diogenes Allen puts the matter as follows:

> We may ask, "Is there a reason for the order of the universe?" and get two types of answer. One is to go outside the universe to account for its order; another is to account for its order by scientific explanations and perhaps in addition metaphysical ones which remain within the universe. In either case the question is answered. But with the question of *existence* of the universe, we do not know whether there is a reason for its existence or not. It is not a matter of a dispute over what the reason is, or of the type of reasons required, as with the order of the universe; in this case we do not know whether or not there is a reason for the *existence* of the universe.[6]

When, that is to say, one cannot ever dismiss from his mind that childlike but not childish question which has forever been the primal forest of wonder, "Why is there something rather than nothing?" the multivaried and detailed rejoinder of the descriptive sciences that things that are seem to be constructed in such and such a way, and seem to operate in such and such predictable regularities, etc., etc., quite misses the point. Or if, as is likely the case, the researcher in the natural sciences and, often, the philosopher say of the question that it is a "useless question," they should not be surprised that many in our time who retain a primal curiosity about total-meaning, dismiss their dismissal as a perilous sickness. These others come to a conclusion, so clearly articulated in the literature, art, and drama of this generation, that if that question should cease to form, define, and ever freshly reconstitute the human person, then mankind is indeed an absurdity, a "useless passion," an exquisitely bitter joke of cosmic proportions. For, says Professor Allen, "One is not asking how the universe operates or why the universe operates as it does, but what its status is;

one is concerned to know whether it is ultimate or not, regardless of its ways of operating and its contents."[7]

The question about the status of the universe, so airily dismissed in the days of the regnancy of the logical positivists, is returning to roost again among the philosophical fraternity. But no answer seems to be forthcoming. "We cannot specify why the totality should have a reason for its existence, but on the other hand there is nothing known to preclude it from having a reason."[8]

If, then, one is to advance beyond the incessant question, "Is the universe ultimate or not?" the question must be raised in the company and context of other considerations. In the final chapter I shall suggest such considerations and propose a context which has a size and nature appropriate to the question. Such suggestions will not, to be sure, make it logically necessary to conclude that the universe is not ultimate, that the universe is indeed dependent. But they will be, I think, such clear and reasonable "suasions" as to invite the mind to suppose that the universe may be dependent, and give universe-intrinsic grounds for that judgment.

## Grace, Its Content in Nature and in History

Just as, then, a "sense for the world" is prevented from gathering appropriate fullness because of the logically unwarranted assumption that the independence of the universe is scientifically verifiable, a second impedient oversimplification must also be considered.

The issue can be put thus: the phrase "a sense for the world" proposes reflection about the double context within which all acts of perception and reflection take place. The huge categories, nature and history, are no longer clearly defined or capable of being cleanly set over against each other. If by history we mean most simply the realm of human action, and if by nature we mean the not-self as the given theatre within which such actions occur, then it is clear that as historical life witnesses broad and deep advances

in knowledge about and interference with natural life the inter-
penetrative and modifying energies of this transaction will present
an ever more subtle situation. And the appropriateness of the
relatively distinct older use of the theological categories of nature
and of grace will have to follow the facts and reformulate their
meanings. The suggestion here is that practical anthropocentrism,
the tyranny of the historical, may arise and take command with so
olympian a certainty that the world-as-nature actually ceases to
impact upon consciousness with steady force. Professor Loren
Eiseley writes:

> There is something wrong with our world view. It is still Ptole-
> maic, though the sun is no longer believed to revolve around the
> earth.

> We teach the past, we see further backward into time than any
> race before us, but we stop at the present, or at best, we project far
> into the future idealized versions of ourselves. All that long way
> behind us we see, perhaps inevitably, through human eyes alone. We
> see ourselves as the culmination and the end, and if we do indeed
> consider our passing, we think that sunlight will go with us and the
> earth be dark. We are the end. For us continents rose and fell, for
> us the waters and the air were mastered, for us the great living web
> has pulsated and grown more intricate.[9]

Most cultural history of Western reflection since the Enlightenment obscures the truth of that observation in efforts to disclose
it. For such studies assume that the world-as-nature, following the
work and thought of Galileo and Copernicus, has been the focal
point of man's attention. It is precisely the vigor of this investiga-
ting, systematizing, describing, and ultimately, the practical utilizing for man's purposes of the energies and processes of nature,
which permit, indeed invite, this misunderstanding. That vast intellectual energies of post-Enlightenment man have gone into investigations of natural fact must not seduce us into the assumption that
nature as such retains its actuality, force, and fundamental character as the determining reality of modern reflection. Nature as field

of intellectual and instrumental operations is, indeed, the focus, both as material for reflection and as productive of a methodology for control. But in this process nature as a primal reality is subsumed under *nature as resource for historical transformation.* The central, operating factor in world-reflection since the Enlightenment has not been the world-as-nature; it has rather been the world-as-history, as this world, with man its primary agent, has been instrumentally anthropocentrized in fact.

Modern anthropocentrism has arisen as a function of this vast accomplishment of man-as-history operating *upon* nature; the life of nature has been drawn up into the volitional and fatefully decisional life of man-as-history. It is within the whorls of man's fiercely expanding managerial activity as historical actor that nature now presents itself to man for reflection.

But it is an illusion that man, in such a reflective life inclusive of rationalized, ordered, and used nature is really admitting the "creation" as such into his reflections. It is a fallacy to suppose that because we know about and think about atoms, genes, astrophysical space and organization we are thereby thinking about the creation. That fallacy arose out of the ironical fact that human exuberance about the knowledge of and control of aspects of nature has really little to do with nature-as-creation. *Creation* is a religious and philosophical term; it is not a term whose proper reference is simply the fact of, or the possible structure and process of, the world. The term "creation" contains and requires a God-postulation. Until we get this through our heads, and admit nature as the *creation* into our reflective nexus, and permit nature there to retain its intransigent reality, we shall neither theologize soberly nor be theologically guided to act constructively. Is it not likely that the reality of death—the event of it presently turned over to morticians, and grave reflection about it relegated to the comparative obscurity of poets and short story writers—has become in popular culture a dirty cheat, a surprise, almost an illegal and unmannerly interruption of the carefully planned party *because* the inexorable periodicity of the world-as-nature has been muted by the drama of man's historical accomplishments?

Several years ago Michael Harrington, engaged in a round-table discussion of current utopian ideas, recalled the epigram of a Russian revolutionary thinker to the effect that "the function of socialism is to raise men from the level of a fate to that of a tragedy," and added:

> . . . Utopia is not going to solve everything by any means. As a matter of fact, I have thought for a long time about Marx's prediction that in a society where men are no longer murdered or starved by nature, but where nature is under man's control there would be no need of God because God is essentially man's projection of his own fears and hopes—a curious image. In contrast to that, I wonder whether, at precisely the moment all economic problems disappear, there could not be a great *growth* in religion rather than a decline. It is a possibility, because we would have a society in which men would die not from floods or plagues or famines, not from their own idiocies about the economy. They would die from death. And at that point the historical shell around the fact of death would be broken. For the first time society would face up to death itself.[10]

Have not humanistic studies which one might suppose capable of exposing this humorous and ironical diminishment of the nexus of human reflection actually participated in the shrinkage? For these studies, also, anthropocentric and sometimes excruciatingly acute in their exposition of awareness, sensation, and introspection, have invited the mind of modernity to fold itself inward upon its own and its fellows' cerebral and emotional past and present, and by the very virtuosity of that accomplishment diminished the reality of unregarding and ever-persistent nature. The questions men ask (and in theology the questions God puts) are thus dealt with by a reflective capacity shrivelled by the very attentions which constitute its pride.

Let us as an exercise in imagination suppose that one curiously unshrunk in primal naiveté falls into reflection while standing in the midst of a great, proud, modern city. Its very form, structure, vigorous systematic of production, consumption, and communication, is a microcosm of a triumphant technology fashioned upon scientific knowledge as its base. Let one suppose further that by catastrophe or plague all human life were in a moment annihilated. Within decades all the piled-up accomplishments of man would fall into dissolution—rotted, fallen into debris, dissolved, their slowly disappearing remnants covered over by the creeping greenness of a fecund and luxurious nature. Chartres would become a squat mound with vines entwined about broken fragments of interesting shapes, and Rembrandt canvasses soggy strips of fungus-splotched fiber. The waters of the man-defiled Rhine, Hudson, and Thames would run again to the sea sparkling and clean and their banks resound to the calls of the returning birds.

If men accept an understanding of the world as independent, there is no place for God's agency, and the notion of grace is not credible; if men so radically historicize their understanding of the world as to bring all dynamics of world-happening within the orbit of man's determination, there is no place for God's agency, and the notion of grace is not credible. Further, if men's sense of reality, identity, worth, and function is overwhelmingly defined by their place and role and function within the world-as-nature *technologically* organized, a third force is at work to transform their sense for the world.

Perhaps a new designation is needed to point to the dominant sensibility of men as they are defined, and are tempted to define themselves within a technologically organized world. The entire world, to be sure, is not so organized; but the parts and peoples of it that are not seem to wish they were. "Undeveloped" is the term used to describe them.

In seeking for such a new designation one remembers how men of other times have generalized about the particularity of the human species. He has been called *Homo sapiens*, the creature who reflects; or *Homo politicus*, the creature who creates institutions,

makes laws, and orders the powers of life for public purposes; or
*Homo faber*, the creature who makes tools to extend his powers
and multiply his hands; or *Homo ludens*, the creature who, standing apart from himself, can be amused by himself.

But many a new man of our new time might be designated as
*Homo operator*. His procedures are often at a distance, removed
from actual things, persons, purposes. He sits at a desk covered
with papers that represent things, not at a bench covered with
real things. Actualities come before him in their mathematized
or otherwise symbolized equivalents. He is teller, broker, retailer,
distributor, operator of a part of a system. He sits in an office in
Boston and sells State of Maine potatoes, which he has never seen,
to a wholesaler who is an "account" and a voice on the telephone
and who lives in Chicago. He crouches over levers of a crane and
guides it to lift stone from Indiana, which he has never touched,
to the top of a construction job in Omaha, where it is fixed in
walls he need not look at, designed for purposes he has nothing to
do with, by men whose names he does not know and whose faces
he never sees.

The pilot of a modern aircraft is *Homo operator* in an almost
absolute sense. Every natural reality that makes his plane go and
holds it up arrives to his sense and procedure via gauges, indica-
tors, lights, and meters. *Numbers* tell him the state of his airy
world: elevation, velocity, the condition or status of engine, wing,
tail, fuel, and water. Distance is transposed into time: Atlanta is
ninety minutes from Chicago. Visual fact is transposed into interpretive signals on a dial; the actual, and the responses necessary
to conform to it, is taken out of the agency of personal judgment
and transferred to computerized adjustments appropriate to a
complex of factors that require neither hands nor eyes.

The point here has nothing to do with the value, trustworthiness,
or even the necessity of such instrumentation of natural fact. The
point is rather to enforce the truth of the argument that technology
as such, and quite apart from one's assessment of its promises and

perils, profoundly changes *Homo operator*'s sense for the world. One is reminded of Professor Paul Tillich's "technical reason," which provides means for ends but provides no guidance for the determination of ends. Production, or plain continued operations, become frantically involved with ever more sophisticated means, and the tools which are used in the process create a "second nature" above physical nature which subjects man to itself, and proves as unpredictable and destructive as nature itself. Indeed, there have been perceptive questions as to why the recent vehement determination of the young to change the priorities of America's national life has so precipitously collapsed. The force of Professor Tillich's assertion that technology injects a "second nature" into man's reflective life is certified by a typical student outburst: "What can we do? Where can we grab hold of what's fixed and set and rolling along? The whole damned thing has a life of its own; it runs by itself!"

This changed sense for the world demands two quite fresh responses to a world so organized in mind and practice.

The first of these is a vast expansion of the notion of nature itself. For the reference of the term must now go beyond the given nonhuman world of land and sea and forest and wind and rain and petroleum and the entire range of plant and animal life. *Homo operator* is as ultimately dependent upon this primal nature as man has always been; but the *sense* for this dependence is distanced and muted in virtue of the astounding transformations science-based technology has wrought. The "made" world that has come into being following the work of the chemist, the physicist, the biologist, the engineer, is closer to the common life of the millions than the "natural" world of his fathers. Forests meet him as paper and plywood; oil and coal as energy, saran wrap, tires, and pharmaceuticals.

Nor can the argument that this transformed, artifactual world constitutes a primary factor in contemporary estrangement really be sustained. There is estrangement, to be sure, but observation forces one to locate its causes elsewhere. For so adaptable is man to the world that science has made possible and technology has realized that in this new, "made," extrapolated world most men feel at home. Here he "belongs," in the company of fellow operators in the world he finds his "natural" community; here he feels secure, for he knows the rules of the game; here he sees and works with astounding fabrications out of primal nature and deals with them with familiar, even playful, recognition.[11]

If, then, we are required to expand our notion of the natural to include man's transformation of it, we are also required to relate grace to nature in ways appropriate and adequate to nature so understood and so brought within man's operational existence. The advancement of this theological task cannot be accomplished by theology working in a specialized, reconceptualizing disengagement from other areas of men's sensibility.

For the reality of grace must be encountered, specified, named, and known in *whatever* perceptions carry upon and within themselves the impact and quality that resonates back to that fountain, origin, and actor-in-grace who, in the tradition, is called ". . . the God of Abraham, Isaac and Jacob . . ." and ". . . the Father of our Lord Jesus Christ." This interior resonance of recognition, begetting, or evoking praise and thanksgiving, is a function of the particularity of grace itself. For grace has its marks. Whenever men encounter grace it is the shock and the over-plus of sheer gratuity that announces the presence, as indeed, it invented the name. By gratuity is meant a primal surprise, the need-not-have-been of uncalculated and incalculable givenness. "Amazing" is the only adequate adjective; wonder is the ambience. For amazement, wonder, and grace occur together. ". . . they were amazed at the graciousness of his words. . . ."

But the very capacity for wonder can become calloused, covered over with the scar tissue that forms when experience abounds in the new, the marvelous, the fantastic. Operational man presents a hard case for the voices in our day that plead for a "rebirth of wonder." A generation reared on the T.V. extravaganza has been so visually and aurally bombed and banalized that efforts to reach and touch into life the shrunken sense of gratuity must find fresh ways. There can be no doubt that the church, the community that lives by the recognition of grace, is beginning to understand this and grope for such ways as shall celebrate the "difference" in her sense for the world, and signalize this known difference by exterior signs. The movement is all in one direction—to announce the amazing in, with, and under the common; to beckon to wonder via the close and the usual; to divest the wonderful of the habiliments of elegance and reclothe adoration in simplicity. In architecture the churches cannot out-big the world; therefore the direct, the honest, the unostentatious. In vestments the church cannot outdo Countess Mara; therefore the plain bluntness of common texture. In the language of worship the church cannot longer allure by sonorities of the half-understood; therefore the crispness of clear statement. There is a student congregation known to me in which the general prayer is responded to no longer with the traditional "Amen" but by the rejoinder "We really mean it!"

This moment toward the domestication of the occasions of grace is neither a denial of its source in God nor a diminishment of its power; it is rather a relocation of the encounter amidst those operations which constitute the level-usualness of lived reality. It is a fresh realization of the deeply evangelical truth that the Incarnation of grace, precise in a person, is creative of a sense for the world which is total in its scope, near at hand in its invitation to recognition, adoration, and service, and beseeches and judges us in infinite love through the mortal eyes of human need.

The critical problem of Jesus' use of the "Son of man" term cannot be used to evade the terrible clarity of Matthew 25:31 ff. For it is God the Father who here assesses and judges. When the Father's blessing is declared upon those who cared for the hungry, thirsty, lonely, naked, sick, imprisoned, and when, astonished, men asked where and when it was that the Father was thus encountered, the identification of a gracious God with the anguish of men is absolute. "I tell you this: anything you did for one of my brothers here, however humble, you did for me."

To relegate this saying to the field of ethics is a fateful misunderstanding. For the reality of grace is not severable from that web and bundle of life out of which the human emerges and is defined, within which the negatives of need and anguish and death, as well as the affirmative vitalities of beauty and joy burst forth, to which the Incarnation of grace came, and which, in the numberless occasions of experience, constitutes the theatre of man's redemption by grace.

## Grace and Man's Identity

In this section we shall inquire what relation may actually exist between the grace of God and man's sense of identity. The task may well be opened by recalling an aphorism of Professor Karl Rahner, variations of which occur often and with growing enrichment of meaning throughout the accumulating volumes of his *Theological Investigations*.[12] "All truth cannot be less than the truth that specifies my being."

It is certainly true that a capital fact that "specifies my being" is simply that a person is not a person by himself. My late colleague, Professor Joseph Haroutunian gave the last years of his dedicated life to a criticizing of the Christian vocabulary by bringing central terms under the disclosive illumination of that fact. He wrote as follows:

> We must take another look at "human nature" upon which the grace of God or God himself is said to act. It is not at all obvious that *human* nature or humanity is what a man is born with, so that one can study and describe it as the individual's private equipment. We know human beings in actual intercourse with their environment and in their actual communion with their fellowmen. Characteristic activities of human beings, such as speech, thinking, willing, loving, and hating, do not occur and are unthinkable apart

from an interpersonal setting. Even perceptions, feelings, emotions, and actions occur in a social context, and these are what they are as responses in the common life men have with their fellows.

. . . We have no ontological status prior to and apart from communion. Communion is our being; the being we participate in is communion, and we derive our concrete selves from our communion. The old controversy between the realists and the nominalists about universals and particulars is incongruous with the ontology of communion. We have to do, not with universals, but with our neighbors, not with particulars, but with particular fellowmen. We do not participate individually in Being, and Being is not by our own being individually. There is no individual to participate in Being or to make Being to be. In the beginning, by God's creation, is the *fellowman*, and the fellowman is by loving his neighbor. The apparently universal notion, at least in the Western world, that *one* man can *be* and that he can have a nature suggests an alienation that gives us, not a *human* ontology, but one from which the human manner of being is excluded. In the beginning is communion and not being or Being. For this reason, in Christian philosophy, traditional ontology is a source of misunderstanding and confusion.[13]

Just as the understanding of the self must be pervaded by the knowledge that selfhood as a notion is incapable of specification except as the fellow self in communion with selves, a second contextual matrix for the achievement of identity must be grasped with equal resolution and insight. The natural world, within which men thus socialized in self-understanding actualize their being, must be acknowledged not simply as "out there" but a self-constituting datum operative in deep and steady interiority.[14]

The explication of interiority entails recollection and illustration. When, for instance, I consider my life and the million-faced coruscations of meaning, illusive but unforgettable, which light up or break out of the sheer factic *thereness* of the physical world, I am astounded by the number and the force of them. They include childhood's personification of animals and trees and clouds and all dumb things; the relentless allure of the sea in Homer, in Melville, in Conrad; Shakespeare's use of analogies from nature to pierce to the heart of the pathos of passingness:

> That time of year thou mayst in me behold
> When yellow leaves, or none, or few, do hang
> Along those boughs which shake against the cold,
> Bare ruin'd choirs where late the sweet birds sang.

Does it mean nothing for our reality as persons that the natural world which is not human is yet *to* the human a life-sustaining placenta of self-consciousness? Is it without force that metaphors drawn from that world have been immemorially necessary when men have sought to find a language ample enough and powerful enough to celebrate or lament the "glories of our blood and state"? John Milton was quite clear about the Reformation doctrine of grace; he was quite aware that nightingales are not sources of grace. He was also quite certain that the God of grace encountered in redemption was not without such manifestations of care and beauty in the world of the creation as to constitute it an occasion of grace. And therefore:

> Now came still evening on, and twilight gray
> Had in her sober livery all things clad;
> Silence accompanied, for beast and bird,
> They to their grassy couch, these to their nests.
> Were slunk, all but the wakeful nightingale;
> She all night long her amorous descant sung
> > (*Paradise Lost*, Book IV, lines 598 f.) .

In an earlier chapter, reference was made to the enigmatic verses (19–25) in the eighth chapter of the Epistle to the Romans. The amount of exegetical perspiration that has been exuded in Protestant efforts to privatize and spiritualize these verses, to make them exclusively cultic and ecclesiastical, has all the marks of a dogmatic tradition whipping recalcitrant dogs into line. Why should holy meaning be so dogmatically restricted to the *historical* drama of life as presumptuously to sweep clean of meaning the entire vast, cosmic, all-engendering, and all-enfolding matrix without which that life is literally inconceivable?

Paul made no such effort; and while there is in Paul no developed theology for nature, there is, in this *loci* and elsewhere, just such "an opening of the mind toward possibility" as demands that postbiblical reflection for which Professor Ricoeur (as quoted earlier) so urgently calls.

The scope of the salvific force of grace may be affirmed as identical with the creation by reflection upon the condition set by the very structure of personal identity. That structure specifies what are the interior possibilities of that "consummation" that faith is promised. For *consummation* of identity must be in some relation to the *constitution* of identity. It follows that inasmuch and insofar as man's transactions with nature, spiritual and operational, are powerful constituents of identity, the consummation of life in Eternal Life cannot annul or structurally distort the very constitution of life. By "constitution" is here meant not the accidents or individual fortunes that affect my personal history, but rather those primary relations, appetites, needs, self-disclosing and self-maturing factors that constitute the human as such.

Even a consummation that goes beyond "what ear hath heard or eye seen" cannot so absolutely transcend in elevation or amplitude as to be utterly discontinuous with these structural factors of the personal. Otherwise consummation would not be consummation; it would be rather so totally a "new being" as to be unrecognizable by the historical being who, *in* the world of the creation and the divine redemption, learned to envision, and to long for newness of life and consummation.

Redemption means life with God. Faith means to accept what God gives, himself as giver and himself as the gift. To be a Christian means to accept, know, enjoy, and live on this acceptance of our acceptance. This acceptance of an accepted life is not bestowed, known, experienced, or loved in capsulated privacy; the very structure of knowledge, experience, and love close that possibility. This redeemed-life is given and matured in time and space and matter, among my fellow creatures, human and nonhuman. One cannot speak of this life apart from participating in and receiving identity-forming powers from those orderings of community, symbolizations of meaning, conceptual accruals and specifications of form and substance and energy which make up the actual life of intellection.[15] As a man-participant and inheritor of all this, I announce my "membership" in a body which is trans-self in all delighted or mordant moments of recognition which occur when, in literature, art, and music, I find formal distillations of curiosity, creativity, loss, gain, ambiguity, frustration, play, fear, love, hate, hope, and far-dreaming.

This life I have as redeemed into life-with-God is Eternal Life. I have it now; it will never cease to be. If one is redeemed he is "hidden with Christ in God," and God does not die. When, therefore, I am saddened by the knowledge of my mortality, that sadness is both real and qualified. I am saddened by the understandable regret that so significant a person as I am should cease to enliven mortal history. But the sadness is decisively qualified by the center of faith—that the redeemed are with God, and that God does not die.

But what could such an eternal life with and in God possibly mean for a person whose personhood came to be, and is, as a total function of residency in the total creation?

It follows from the logic of life in the only way the term has meaning for a person, that the entire creation—within which and as a part of which I *am*, have an identity, and without which I cannot conceive of being an identity at all, but only an emptily potential entity—must be the sufficient object of the divine redemption. It follows that for a person among persons and things, redemption into a world-of-relations of some transformed relational-complex is the only possibility of redemption that can have meaning, value, and fulfillment, or even interest.

Because men exist and are as relational entities, only a redemption *among* can be a real redemption. Only, that is to say, when the meaning and act of redemption is within the web of creation can a salvable identity be "saved" in any sense that makes sense. It is only in such a self-world context that I have a body, a mind, a memory, a spirit, expectation, response. What and who might be a person apart from this web? A no-thing.[16]

The redemption of the *world* must be permitted to mean what it says, or it will cease to mean anything meaningful. In a bluntly human sense *my* redemption must include the possibility of redemption of everything. For I am no-thing apart from everything. The poet Richard Wilbur asks:

> . . . What should we be without
> The dolphin's arc, the dove's return,
>
> These things in which we have seen ourselves and spoken?
> Ask us, prophet, how we shall call
> Our natures forth when that live tongue is all
> Dispelled, that glass obscured or broken
>
> In which we have said the rose of our love and the clean
> Horse of our courage, in which beheld
> The singing locust of the soul unshelled,
> And all we mean or wish to mean.[17]

# 6.

# Christian Theology and the Environment

The preceding chapters are among the things I have thought, recalled from tradition, and have been forced to reassess en route to the concrete and urgent matter which is the substance of this chapter. The environmental problem, that is to say, has been the issue that started and powered the reflections there recorded about God, Christ, Grace, and the interpretation of Scripture. In this closing chapter the relation between environmental fact and Christian ethics, and the grace of God, must be more tightly drawn. That effort will be made under two headings.

## The Context of Ethical Discourse

Fundamental ethical categories—responsibility, obedience, love, integrity, and others—have not lost their Christian imperative force. But as the range and context of contemporary man in knowledge and operation has steadily widened, the setting of ethical reflection, the options open to decision, and the complexity of the facts that must be respected in the act of decision have multiplied. The physician treating illness has at his command therapeutical and procedural devices that no previous age has had, and his decisional situation is thereby complicated.[1] In every field of science and technology, ecological fact is presently so clear and the results of its ignoring so catastrophic that older guides to action are either useless or positively perilous. Sociology, which is but the ecological understanding of man's life among and within groups and institutions, is quite aware of the uncalculated and perhaps incalculable tremors that originate in private and group action and profoundly modify areas of life distant from that originating center. Psychological studies have long since gone far beyond experimental work in perception, sensation, memory, etc., and have so rooted the beheld data in familial and other primary contexts that these researches are an illustration of the fundamental postulate of ecology—that anything is related to everything. The very *field* of ethical reflection is in ever more complex and intraactive motion.

Nor is this expansion of field the only factor that constitutes the difficulty for contemporary Christian ethics. The traditional center of such reflections remains the center—the reality of God and his will as embodied in and illuminated by Jesus Christ. But that force and figure is clearer as *center* than as content-for-ethics. Biblical and historical studies have made clear that (a) there is probably no historical or other road to the precise recovery of the "intention" of Jesus; (b) that what we can be quite clear about because it seems most general and pervasive is that that "intention" was an eschatological act and message for and about the kingdom of God.

But even that relative clarity exacerbates the problem of defining what might be for us in our time a "starting point" for a Christian ethics centered upon Jesus. The "eschatological" as a formative ambience for faithful self-definition and action, as this worked in an earlier period to organize thought about the relation of God to time and space and history and nature, is not easily translatable into the mind of an era that lives ever more consciously out of knowledge of beginnings, developments, forces, and transformations, ascribes absolute agency to immanental vitalities, and understands destiny to be a secret folded within the coils of human history within the vast theatre of cosmos.

This historical distancing from originating events begot a process of demythologizing into various categories—subjective interiority, radical symbolization, etc. The entire movement has had a profound effect that is designated by the title of this section, "The

Context of Ethical Discourse." And necessarily; for the fortunes of men's minds follow the fortunes of their bodies with absolute seriousness; their reflections reenact the orbits of their operations. When men's bodies walk upon the moon their questions about the meaning and intention of Jesus, and of faith's Christ, will not be content to swing within the older orbits of self, family, nation, church, or even the "historical" as exemplified by the career of humanity as a particular species busily managing or mismanaging life in the thin biosphere that surrounds a particular heavenly body. Men seek patterns of meaning that are correlative in scope to the magnitude of their questions.

We may, to be sure, so "historicize" reality as to shrink its data to a size more comfortable for our anthropocentric inclinations. But such a decision is counterproductive for our children, who, for better or worse, *do* have their hands upon the very large—in astrophysical investigations—and upon the very small—in subatomic and genetic researches.[2] A generation whose "world" is of that size and complexity, and known to be bound together in an ecological web of some astonishing subtlety, will not cease to ask about God and Christ and grace in terms that have an equivalent magnitude.[3]

It will not suffice for the present scope of meaning-reflection to deal with a world so known (however imperfectly) by appeals to the New Testament's clear distinction between the world as cosmos and the world as historical drama (*kosmos* and *aion*). Both nature and history are mute as regards God and meaning; and the life of nature has been so drawn up into the energies of history in virtue of man's science-based manipulations of nature, that these categories, useful and legitimate in the biblical world view, are no longer of the same categorical efficiency.

Nor will it do, either, to elaborate on ethics that bows in the direction of the good that is made possible for individuals and society by modern "operational" man, but does not take seriously the absolute necessity to relate the grace of God to the disclosure of this good and men's joy in it. *Theological* ethics, that is to say, must address man in his strength as well as his weakness, in his joy as well as his sorrow, and in his accomplishments—to direct them and hold them in proportion to larger goods—as well as in his failures—to forgive and console them.

When men experience as a positive good the activities of their lives, the range of the work of their brains and imaginations and hands (what they feel in the discovery and reorganization of novel substances and energies and the excitement accompanying the never before put-together), they do not feel either sinful, pretentious, or subhuman. They know, rather, that it is precisely in such work and works that some healthful reality of their nature is being fulfilled in joy and creativity, some significant element in their constitution as men is being realized.

The theological requirement of this anthropological fact is clear and commanding. The grace of joy and creativity, the possibility of life-understanding and life-enhancement thus experienced, the sense of a self-transcending engagement with the allure and power and mystery of the world refuses to be identified as absolutely separate from the grace and joy and new possibility given to human life in that Christically focused grace, greater than all, which is the forgiveness of sin. Precisely here is disclosed the theological and pastoral necessity to speak of the grace of the Triune God in a way that breaks out of the Protestant disposition to enclose the total reality of grace within the focal point of the second article of the doctrine—of Christ and redemption.[4]

For while nature and history may be mute about both the reality of God and meaning in life, man's experiences engender prehensions which become occasions within which the announced presence of a gracious God in the divine redemption is, by a necessary momentum, postulated as the meaning of the creation. Israel's faith produced Deuteronomy (that record of historical occasions when a gracious God was encountered) before it produced Genesis (the story of the creation of the world by God), and that sequence is of significance. It affirms that the God who is man's Redeemer dare not be acknowledged as other or less than the Creator of the world. The scope of Lordship dare not be specified as less than the scope of all that is. Indeed, Psalm 104, firmly fixed in that conviction, is literally a cosmic-ecological doxology.

That faith should forever have to risk the act of investiture of the whole in the power of the experienced redemptive occasion—is this not of the profoundest character of genuine faith? The eighth chapter of Romans tormentedly pushes through to such a conclusion. And more—for precisely in the ambiguity and often hiddenness of the gracious presence of God in nature and in history lies the inexhaustable and generative power of faith. All occasions that promise but do not suffice, and in a way that leaves the power of the promise unabated by the insufficiency, constitute a "negative" testimony to a possibility. Glimpses that unforgettably allure but do not focus into clarity or satisfaction constitute a witness by the very pathos of their partiality. Meanings that beckon, slip, and slide amidst the patterns of history, form a mind and sensibility that can neither dismiss them as of no worth nor combine and accumulate them into the solidarity of certainty. Faith, that is to say, when it becomes maturely conscious of the risk-character of its demand, is always an act of investiture of total reality with that vision, value, and meaning which has been granted to us in our encounters with the deepest, highest, and holiest. When that deepest, highest, and holiest is the presence and power of grace, and when the occasions of its life-sustaining gift are granted to man within his historical life among his fellows as well as within his residency within the nonhuman world-theatre of his existence, the place and scope for the ethical is given along with the realm of the gracious.

This effort to draw our regard for the world-as-nature into organic relation with the reality of grace is not a merely theoretical exercise; its intention is practical. Unless some huge, primarily religious, and commanding vision of the future of the world can seize, release, and exalt our spirits free of our unregarding, arrogant, and ultimately suicidal operations with the creation, we shall continue to be bombarded by the awesome data of ecological disaster, but remain unsupplied with a theological indicative as big as the issue and an ethicality unexpanded to appropriate dimensions.[5]

## Ethicality and Verification

In the course of his journey to Jerusalem he was travelling through the borderlands of Samaria and Galilee. As he was entering a village he was met by ten men with leprosy. They stood some way off and called out to him, "Jesus, Master, take pity on us." When he saw them he said, "Go and show yourselves to the priests"; and while they were on their way they were made clean

(Luke 17:11–14, NEB).

I wake to sleep, and take my waking slow,
I feel my fate in what I cannot fear,
I learn by walking where I have to go.

This shaking keeps me steady, I should know.
What falls away is always, and is near.
I wake to sleep, and take my waking slow.
I learn by going where I have to go.[6]

The New Testament episode and the poem make the same point: action may sensitize cognition. We do not do what we should only after we are clear about all the facts; we also learn about facts when we go the way we must. The doing of the required illuminates and multiplies the possible; it draws the mind forward into fresh cognitions. Walking where one "has to go" discloses hitherto unregarded relations. The incessant pressure of the question, "What ought I to do?" decisively modifies and opens the epistemological question, "What can I know?" The ten lepers were cleansed "on the way" to an indeterminate and clinically absurd obedience. As old as Augustine is the relation between how I regard a thing and what is possible to know about a thing. Love opens to knowledge.

*Non intradit veritatem nisi per caritatem*—there is no entrance to truth save by love.

This symbiotic coexistence and interaction of the risk of faith, the consequent investiture of the creation with a gracious possibility in virtue of the Incarnation of grace in time, space, matter ("born of woman, crucified under Pontius Pilate"), and an ethicizing of our regard for and our transactions with nature as *still*, despite man's rapacity and despoliation, a field of grace—this is proposed as a Christian theological pattern of a magnitude that matches the misery of our environmental debacle.

Can the affirmation that God is gracious, and that God's creation must be enjoyed and used as a gracious gift, have the power to accomplish that radical change in "the spirit of our minds" that the problem of man and environment demands? Two considerations are in order as we ask that question. First, if the Christian community is to go beyond a mere adding of its numerically modest voice to the urging of that issue, that community under the guise of public morality will betray its responsibility. A change in the "spirit of our minds" requires something vastly more than a combination of frightening facts and moral concern. There is sufficient evidence that men are quite capable of marching steadily into disaster fully equipped with the facts. Pride, comfort, and an idolatrous and brutal hardness of heart have for several generations permitted the American nation to stare straight into the face of poverty, injustice, and the calcified privilege of the powerful—and leave national priorities unchallenged.

Against that fact one must assess realistically the sanguine assumption that knowledge of fact can by itself create change. Fundamental changes are evaded by the dramatization of small ones; faults at the center of a system are obscured or dismissed by cosmetic operations on the surface. A political and an economic system develops a rhetoric of celebration about its accomplishments that is capable of an act of seduction on a national scale. Rigor mortis is celebrated as stability.

Ecological rationality, and the creation of public law appropriate to justice and care for the clear and clamant needs of persons— these right ends of social purpose are regularly shattered against inherited and clearly no longer effective laws governing uses of property, the exercise of legally defended autonomy in land use, and definitions of corporate responsibility bent to the advantage of the strong.

The second consideration is this: the Christian community exists in the power of events, presences, and visions that are betrayed when its total and holy understanding of man and God, man and the neighbor, man and God's creation are translated down from their fiercely elevated and dynamic, steadily revolutionary reality. That the care of the earth is rational, necessary, aesthetic —the convulsive and renovating and never-to-be-quieted torment and glory of the story of God and Abraham, God and Jesus Christ, God and our recalcitrant spirits—does not have to be invoked for *that*. The community of the people of God, who live by and are held within God's grace has another and wilder thing to do. They are a people caught and held by a vision of a King, a kingdom, and a consummation—and by the massive contexts of culture, history, nature, as fields of its holy disturbance.

It is not an accidental fact that utopias have been formulated only where the historical dynamism inseparable from Christian faith has been exercised. But there is a decisive difference between utopias and the visions of human life and possibility that the faith relentlessly explodes into fresh forms. Utopias owe their character and force to the vigor of the "see what is possible!"

The Christian vision is fundamentally different; its vision of what is possible is engendered both by the realities of human existence and the promises of the God of its faith. Christian vision believes out of both possibility and promise. Its fundamental trust is not in the allure or energy of the possible (these collapse, wane, frustrate) but in the Giver and Promiser who does not abandon what he has given or renounce his promises. Just as one's hope for eternal life in God is a correlate of the reality of the promises of the God of his faith, and does not ultimately rest upon either man's desire or man's hope—so man's vision of the New Creation is a product of God who is affirmed in faith to be a Creator of the world, Redeemer of the world, and Sanctifier of the world.

The one comprehensive reality of this Trinitarian God is grace; the place of encounter with this grace of the Triune God is the given and modified arena of creation, the alienated arena of redemption, the envisioned arena of the future of man, the Spirit, and the world.[7] It is in the power of that argument that this entire effort has been undertaken.

Is there, however, apart from the sheer momentum inherent in the reality of grace itself, and the formal necessity to postulate the grace of the one God as present and at work in the work and presence of the one God, evidence from the facts of life that faith's investiture of everything experienced and reflected about with the supreme meaning-as-grace is an intelligible act?

The theme of this final section is ethicality and verification. By ethicality is meant the necessity for the organization of life toward continuation, care, and enhancement if life is to be at all. That life is like that and that its fundamental drive is in that direction I take to be a nonarguable datum. When in Chapter 5 it was argued that knowledge about the structure and process of the universe does not preclude reflection about the status of the universe— dependent upon God or not—an issue was raised which, regardless of what scientist or philosopher may think, cannot be left hanging for faith. When grace is postulated as the reality of God, as the reality of the life of the Father in the Son, witnessed to by the "internal testimony of the Holy Spirit," then literally all that is must be invested with an interpretation congruent with that postulate. By ethicality, then, is meant not only a way of acting in accord with and as an actualization of that faith, but a way of understanding that begets the possibility to assess all things from that center.

By verification is meant a warrant for the adequacy, coherence, and truth of such an understanding.[8] What warrant is there for such a faith-investiture? What evidence from the world of fact invites the mind to suppose and supports the mind in supposing that the grace of the Creator is a principle of the creation; that a primal regard for things in terms of the marvel and particularity of their "being there" at all is somewhat more than an imposition, or an unwarranted extrapolation from the superheated theological fancy untroubled by intrusions of verifiable fact?

If things cannot continue to be at all except men deal with them with due regard for their given structure and need, then there is certainly rational warrant that assessment of things according to their transutilitarian "good" is an appropriate recognition of an intrinsic "good" in things that are. If a postulate about the source, status, and transpersonal actuality of the world-as-nature (that it is of God, and a theatre of his grace) begets an assessment of that world and a consequent use of it consistent with the assessment then, by an empiricism-of-outcomes, the postulate is logically and experientially warranted. Or, to put the proposal another way: what is necessary for the continued existence of things and essential to prevent the perversion or distortion of the given nature of things may be reasonably postulated as congruent with the truth of things. Indeed this "postulate" moves toward the status of a principle if conditions for the very existence of men and things are *absolute* conditions.

If the realm of nature is regarded and used under the rubric of grace, and responds as if one had discovered her true name, and along with God's human creation "delights" to have a name and to have been given freedom to be, the ancient image of "the morning stars sang together, and all the sons of God shouted for joy" returns with something more than poetic force. If, for instance, Lake Michigan is assessed according to its given ecological structure as a place for multiple forms of life, by nature self-sustaining and clean, available for right use and delight, then in a blunt and verifiable way we are "justified" by grace even in our relation to the things of nature. The opposite of justification is condemnation, and there is an empirically verifiable condemnation that works out its slow but implacable judgment in the absence of such "gracious" regard for nature. If a lake becomes a disposal-resource, or a dump, or a source for water to cool ingots with, or a bath to flush out oil-bunkers (both instances proper to legitimate use and technically subject to restoration to cleanliness) then a repudiated grace that "justifies" becomes the silent agent of condemnation.[9]

> For he has made known to us in all wisdom and insight the mystery of his will, according to his purpose which he set forth in Christ, as a plan for the fullness of time, to unite all things in him, things in heaven and things on earth (Eph. 1:9–10).

# Notes

## Introduction

1. George Santayana, *Poems* (New York: Chas. Scribner's Sons, 1923), p. 2.
2. William James, "Reflex Action and Theism," in *The Limits of Language*, ed. Walker Gibson (New York: Hill and Wang, 1962), pp. 8–9.

## 1. The Emergence of a Theme

1. Joseph Sittler, "Called to Unity," *Ecumenical Review* 14, no. 2 (January 1962): 175–87.
2. Ibid.
3. For a detailed documentation of this discussion see the unpublished doctoral dissertation of Conrad Simonson, "Faith and Order Christology" (University of Chicago, December 1970).
4. Lukas Vischer, "The Faith and Order Movement at the Beginning of a New Period," *Midstream* 4, no. 2 (Winter 1964): 13.
5. Paper No. 44, Commission on Faith and Order, World Council of Churches, Geneva, 1965, p. 43.
6. The expected second volume of Professor Jaroslav Pelikan's *The Christian Tradition* (Volume I, *The Emergence of the Catholic Tradition* [Chicago: University of Chicago Press, 1971]) will quite certainly correct this situation. Its title is *The Spirit of Eastern Christendom*.
7. Joseph Haroutunian, *God With Us* (Philadelphia: Westminster Press, 1965), p. 136.

## 2. Grace in the Scriptures

1. Joseph Sittler, *The Anguish of Preaching* (Philadelphia: Fortress Press, 1966), chap. II.
2. Ernst Käsemann, *New Testament Questions of Today* (Philadelphia: Fortress Press, 1969), p. 62.

3. Allan Galloway, *The Cosmic Christ* (London: Nisbet and Co., Ltd., 1951), p. 54.

4. Amos Wilder, *The Language of the Gospel* (New York: Harper and Row, 1964), p. 37.

5. H. Wheeler Robinson, *Inspiration and Revelation in the Old Testament* (Oxford: Clarendon Press, 1946), p. 1.

6. Cf. the relevant sections in Gerhard von Rad, *Theology of the Old Testament* (New York: Harper and Row, 1965), and the article *"Ktisis,"* in Gerhard Kittel (ed.), *Theological Dictionary of the New Testament*, trans. and ed. Geoffrey W. Bromiley, Vol. III (Grand Rapids: Eerdmans, 1965), pp. 1000 ff.

7. Galloway, *The Cosmic Christ*, pp. 34–35.

8. Paul Ricoeur, "From Existentialism to the Philosophy of Language," *Criterion* 10, no. 3 (Spring 1971): 16.

9. Ibid.

10. Galloway, *The Cosmic Christ*, p. 48.

11. Ibid., p. 49.

## 3. Some Crucial Moments in Ecumenical Christology

1. Emile Mersch, *The Whole Christ* (London: Denis Dobson, 1938), p. 315.

2. Ibid., p. 319.

3. Charles Moeller, *Lumen Vitae*, Vol. 19 (Brussels, 1964), p. 721.

4. Cf. J. Meyendorff, *A Study of Gregory Palamos*, trans. G. Laurence (London, 1964); and V. Lossky, *The Vision of God*, trans. A. Moorhead (London, 1963).

5. Cited by C. Moeller, *Lumen Vitae*, p. 723.

6. The following discussion of Irenaeus is based principally upon two documents: *The Demonstrations of the Apostolic Preaching*, trans. J. Armitage Robinson (New York: Macmillan, 1920); and *Against Heresies*, trans. E. R. Hardy, Library of Christian Classics, Vol. 1 (Philadelphia: Westminster Press, 1953).

But access to the spirit of the Christian East is by no means supplied only by documents! Transdocumentary experience in the worship of the Orthodox churches, whose living piety, practice, and preaching still resonates with an understanding of grace first set forth systematically by Irenaeus—this is the right door to understanding. Lest this devout encounter in worship be too easily dismissed I would call attention to the old aphorism, *Lex orandi, lex credendi*! And further, if one acknowledges the force of the claim that one does not "hear" Shakespeare save in the lively realization of his words as spoken by voices of living men in an actual theatre, it should not be thought strange that the meaning and truth of Irenaeus's teaching about faith's "reenactment" within the believer's life in the web of the created world, and never severed from it, requires the living theatre of the church's worship as the place and precondition for understanding.

7. For a full treatment of Irenaeus's theology, cf. Gustaf Wingren, *Man and the Incarnation* (Philadelphia: Fortress Press, 1959).

8. Mersch, *The Whole Christ*, p. 230.

9. *Service Book and Hymnal* (Philadelphia: The Board of Publication, The Lutheran Church in America, 1958), p. 30.

10. The contemporary theological scene is a veritable convulsion induced by a large number of studies advocating "religionless Christianity," "worldly faith," a faith for man in "The Secular City," and, under the unverifiable proposition that "God is Dead," offering varieties of options. If upon reading these books one has the uneasy feeling that the theme, despite its modern phenomenological data, has been heard before, that feeling might with profit be investigated! And particularly by a generation of theological students who are inclined to suppose that before Schleiermacher the issue of Christian faith and total world-meaning had never been entertained. For when one threads back into apostolic doctrine he finds that the Fathers, too, dared to affirm that if Christ is to be sufficient meaning for anything he must be affirmed in faith as the meaning of everything. The issue was no smaller than that for Irenaeus and, compared with the specious novelty of some who are frantically splashing in the perturbed puddle of secularity, his massive Christology is a masterful feat of navigation.

11. Mersch, *The Whole Christ*, p. 231.

12. Ibid., p. 232.

13. Ibid., p. 233.

14. Ibid., p. 234.

15. Hugo Rahner, *Greek Myths and Christian Mystery* (New York: Harper and Row, 1963), p. 51.

16. Mersch, *The Whole Christ*, p. 264.

17. Jaroslav Pelikan, *The Light of the World* (New York: Harper and Row, 1962), pp. 44 f.

18. P. Evdokimov, *L'Orthodoxie* (Neuchatel: Delachaux et Niestle, 1959); J. Meyendorff, *L'Eglise Orthodoxe hier et aujord'hui* (Paris: Editions du Seuil, 1969); T. Ware, *The Orthodox Church* (Baltimore: Penguin Books, 1959); N. Zernov, *The Church of the Eastern Christians* (New York: Macmillan, 1942); J. Pelikan, *The Spirit of Eastern Christendom*, Vol. 2 of the projected five-volume *The Christian Tradition* (Chicago: University of Chicago Press). Vol. 1, *The Emergence of the Catholic Tradition*, was published in June 1971.

19. C. N. Cochrane, *Christianity and Classical Culture* (New York: Oxford University Press, 1944), pp. 435 f.

20. Ibid., chapters entitled "Regnum Caesaris, Regnum Diaboli," and "Nostra Philosophia."

21. Cf. the article "Theological Table-Talk" by John J. Carey in *Theology Today* 27, no. 3 (October 1970): 315 ff.

22. Ibid., p. 325.

23. Rosemary Reuther, "Critic's Corner," *Theology Today* 27, no. 3 (October 1970): 337.

24. John Black, *The Dominion of Man* (Edinburgh: The University of Edinburgh Press, 1970).

25. At about the time Professor Black's book appeared a headline in the *New York Times* on the day the huge tanker *Manhattan* broke through the hitherto unpenetrated arctic ice, read, "Man's Ancient Enemy Overcome!" This statement is an illustration both of the depth of the perversion that popularly prevails as regards man's living bond to nature, and an instance of what Professor Hugh Iltis of the University of Wisconsin calls "ecological pornography." That a vast and life-preserving ecosystem of ice, tundra, permafrost, and animals, all supportive of an ancient culture and way of life should be regarded as an "enemy to be overcome"—this uncalculated language is witness to a stupor of mind which is more perilous *because* uncalculated.

26. W. H. Auden, "New Year Letter," *The Collected Poetry of W. H. Auden* (New York: Random House, Inc., 1945), p. 270.

## 4. Grace in Post-Reformation Culture

1. Eugene TeSelle, "The Problems of Nature and Grace," *The Journal of Religion* 45, no. 5 (July 1965): 238 ff.

2. It is this relational character of the concept itself which has made even more inappropriate older notions of "infused" grace, "habitual" grace, "regenerative" grace. Such terms sought faithfully to testify to the absolute gratuity of grace, but the language, suggestive of substantial and even subpersonal operations, assumes an ontology that is otiose and an anthropology that is radically inadequate.

3. I shall not argue this conviction. An immense literature discloses that seventeenth and eighteenth century assessments of the Reformation as a virtually detached theological and ecclesiastical phenomenon were followed in the succeeding centuries by studies which radically and justly complicated all simplistic interpretations. This second phase was followed by a third, characterized by new historiographical perspectives and richly supplied with critical editions of the works of the leading reformers. This third phase, honoring and utilizing all the accomplishments of the scholars represented by the second, inaugurated and has sustained a magnificent record of research by scholars

on the continent of Europe, in Great Britain, and in the United States. That the freedom of God in his grace is indeed the core of the complex called "reformation" is admittedly a judgment. But it is a judgment made in knowledge of the enormous labors of one's historical and theological betters, and not in ignorance or defiance of their work.

4. TeSelle, "The Problems of Nature and Grace," p. 238.

5. There is no suggestion here that the great tradition of Roman Catholic theology is to be characterized by what popular understanding and practice actually did with that tradition. Unhappily, however, the depth, balance, and comprehensiveness of a great tradition is not usually maintained across the chasm that separates theological reflection and popular statement, understanding, and practice. The tradition is not justly represented by what Tetzel for instance, preached about sin, merit, or indulgence. But the common people heard Tetzel —not Augustine, Ambrose, or Aquinas.

6. John Addington Symonds, *Renaissance in Italy,* published in 7 vols. between 1875 and 1886. The citation here is from the Modern Library edition (New York, 1935), Vol. 1, pp. 3 f.

7. Cf. Chapter 1, note 1. This statement by the late Professor J. Haroutunian is the bluntest and most succinct I have encountered.

8. This necessity to reflect "beyond" ought properly be explicated. But to do that with the required fullness would entail so extended a detour as virtually to halt the argument. A compromise, full of suggestive force, may be achieved by quoting some sentences from a paper read to a faculty conference in the Divinity School of the University of Chicago by Professor Paul Ricoeur in the Spring of 1971. The statements are such a succinct contribution to the present probing for an adequate principle of interpretation of texts (including the biblical text) that the content of the term "beyond" is given substance and direction.

> The sense of a text is not *behind* the text, but in *front* of it. It is not something hidden, but something *disclosed.* What has to be understood is not the initial situation of discourse, but what points toward a possible world, thanks to the non-ostensive reference of the text. Understanding has less than ever to do with the author and his situation. It wants to grasp the world-propositions opened up by the reference of the text. To understand a text is to follow its movement from sense to reference; from what it says to what it talks about. . . . What we have said about the depth-semantics which structural analysis yields invites us rather to think of the sense of the text as an injunction starting from the text, as a new way of looking at things, as an injunction to think in a certain manner....

> The text speaks of a possible world and of a possible way of orienting oneself within it. The dimensions of this world are properly opened up by, disclosed by the text. Disclosure is the equivalent for written lan-

guage of ostensive reference for spoken language. It goes beyond the mere function of pointing out and of showing what already exists, and in this sense the function of ostensive reference linked to oral language. Here showing is at the same time creating new modes of being.

> . . . it is not the initial discourse situation which has to be understood, but that which, in the non-ostensive reference of the text, points toward a world toward which bursts the reader's situation as well as that of the author. . . . Beyond my situation as reader, beyond the author's situation, I offer myself to the possible modes of being-in-the-world which the text opens up and discovers for me.

9. In Chapter 5 a necessarily fuller and more concrete content is given the meaning of these assertions. The purpose at this point is a "formal" one: to ground the doctrine of grace and such explications as I shall later attempt into those traditional potentials which lie, although neglected, richly in tradition.

10. Alfred North Whitehead, *Adventures of Ideas* (New York: Macmillan, 1933), p. 201.

11. Is it not possible that the twin confessions, the Oneness of God and the Christocentric confession of the Lordship of Christ, might find in a "regional" and "focal point" conceptuality a uniting, discriminating, and clarifying speech which could accomplish for the twentieth century "hearer" of the Word what the metaphysical alliances of the Nicene and Chalcedonian Fathers accomplished for their time and situation? And is it not further possible that the relational-dynamic concepts of contemporary physics and biology might be peculiarly apposite to the uses of biblical language? The God-man relationship in the Bible is regularly in vital terms. God is the source, origin, and fountain of life, food for hunger, water for thirst, restorer of the broken, returner of the lost, redeemer of the enslaved, Savior of the captive, light for darkness, reconciler for alienation. Just as the situation of man is in terms of his being before God in the wrong place, so that works of grace whereby he is placed by God in the right place is not by a hypodermic injection of a "substance" but by an encounter with a possibility that judges misplacement and redeems by restoration. The biblical mode of speech about God and man is relational in fundamental structure and image.

12. In the literature of Christian proclamation known to me there is no more sonorous and astonished apostrophe to this freedom of God in his grace than in the following portion of a sermon preached by John Donne in the year 1627 in London. The quotation is added here for another reason; it illustrates the meaning of the term "occasion" in its theological usage in relation to the freedom of God's grace.

God made Sun and Moon to distinguish seasons, and day, and night, and we cannot have the fruits of the earth but in their seasons: But God hath made no decree to distinguish the seasons of his mercies; In paradise the fruits were ripe, the first minute, and in heaven it is alwaies Autumne, his mercies are ever in their maturity. We ask, *panem quotidianum*, our daily bread, and God never sayes you should have come yesterday, he never sayes you must againe tomorrow, but *today if you will heare his voice*, today he will heare you . . . God (hath) mercy and judgement together: He brought light out of darknesse, not out of a lesser light; he can bring thy Summer out of Winter, though thou have no Spring; though in ways of fortune or understanding, or conscience, thou have been benighted till now, wintered and frozen, clouded and eclipsed, damped and benummed, smothered and stupified till now, now God comes to thee, not as in the dawning of the day, not as in the bud of the spring, but as the Sun at noon to illustrate all shadowes, as the sheaves in harvest to fill all penuries, all occasions invite his mercies, and all times are his season.

13. If there is any consensus at all among the great company of scholars who have given themselves, since the days of Schweitzer, to a reinvestigation of the role of the miracle story in the life and faith of the first century Christian community, it is surely this: that the stories are there because they specify, serve, and characterize the radicality of the "kingdom," and point beyond themselves via the shock of their content to a God-possibility in history which is piously evaded when such stories are made into metaphors of intersubjectivity and its analgesic or salvatory potential, or so "spiritualized" as to make their intent a kind of literary paradigm for untapped human psychological or other resources.

14. There are abundant signs that contemporary reflection, informed by phenomenological ways of analysis, is again becoming aware that the mind does not stop when nothingness is the verdict of its reflection about self and thought and meaning. For *something* is—our environing world encompasses us about with actual beings, structures, and processes. Out of that shock, so Heidegger suggests, comes afresh the surprise of something—"just there," the bald naked thingly givenness of things, and of a world. Out of this proceeds the possibility of what this philosopher calls a "letting-be," a "releasement toward things," a surprised beholding of a world-presented.

15. e. e. cummings, "i thank You God." Copyright © 1950 by e. e. cummings. Reprinted from his volume *Poems: 1923–1954* (New York: Harcourt, Brace and Co., Inc., 1954), p. 464, by permission of Harcourt Brace Jovanovich, Inc.

16. Richard Wilbur, "Objects." From *The Beautiful Changes and Other Poems,* copyright, 1947, by Richard Wilbur. Reprinted by permission of Harcourt Brace Jovanovich, Inc.

## 5. *Grace and a Sense for the World*

1. Condensed from a long paragraph in Sir Arthur Quiller-Couch's volume *The Act of Writing* (New York: G. P. Putnam and Sons, 1916).

2. W. H. Auden, "For the Time Being: A Christmas Oratorio." Copyright © 1945 by W. H. Auden. Reprinted from *The Collected Poetry of W. H. Auden* (New York: Random House, Inc., 1945), p. 411, by permission of the publisher.

3. Joseph Conrad, Preface to *The Nigger of the Narcissus*, in *A Conrad Argosy* (New York: Doubleday, Doran & Company, Inc., 1942), pp. 81–82.

4. Henry James, *The Art of Fiction* (New York: Oxford University Press, 1948), p. 10.

5. This entire section to follow is so directly dependent upon a superb essay ("Theological Reflection on the Natural World," in *Theology Today* 25, no. 4 [January 1969]: 435 ff.) by Professor Diogenes Allen that I shall make slight effort to rephrase what is there so succinctly put, and no effort at all to excuse my eager filching of its argument!

6. Ibid., p. 441.

7. Allen adds, "A conspicuous example of reflection on nature in America is process theology, which has developed largely from the stimulus of Whitehead. Whitehead himself, however, was concerned to understand how the universe operates. To achieve this understanding he found it necessary to postulate God. But his work is still an immanent type of metaphysics; for it is concerned with understanding how the process operates, even though it includes teleological elements in its account; and God, however different he may be from the rest of the universe in his system, is still an item within the universe" (p. 440).

8. Ibid., p. 441.

9. Loren Eiseley, *The Immense Journey* (New York: Vintage Books, 1957), p. 57.

10. Michael Harrington in *Cacotopias and Utopias* (Santa Barbara: The Center for the Study of Democratic Institutions), p. 21. Copyright © 1965 by The Fund for the Republic, Inc.

11. Very responsible descriptions of this process of at-homeness in the technological world are many. For a theological treatment of the matter see Dietrich Von Oppen, *The Age of the Person* (Philadelphia: Fortress Press, 1969). For a sociological study see Victor Ferkiss, *Technological Man* (New York: Braziller, 1969). For a blunt factual account see William Kuhn, *Environmental Man* (New York: Harper and Row, 1969).

But, better still, simply look, feel, think! It is a matter of fact that to the generation born since World War II the outer-space explorations, so dreamlike and mind-boggling to the older generation, have become simply uninteresting. The intersection of many refined technologies represented in these events are, to the younger generation, simply routine, expected, completely "natural" in the sense that each represents another notch in a method of organizing data and energy that is taken for granted.

12. Karl Rahner, *Theological Investigations* (Baltimore: Helicon Press, 1961).

13. Joseph Haroutunian, *God With Us* (Philadelphia: Westminster Press, 1965), pp. 148 ff.

14. The so-called Romantic Movement, ever since the earliest writings of Karl Barth, has been generally regarded as a sub-Christian if not anti-Christian exploration of the human spirit. It is no accident that in these days of awareness of environmental catastrophe the principal figures of that movement—Wordsworth, Coleridge, Hegel, Schelling—should have returned to haunt and trouble the mid-twentieth century intellectual community. For a magnificent discussion of the theological roots of the questions the romantics were asking, and the returning theological relevancy of the relations between selfhood and nature that they were proposing, see W. H. Abrams, *Natural Supernaturalism* (New York: W. W. Norton and Co., 1971).

15. When these essays were in process of formulation I had thought to include among them an extended discussion of the poetry of Gerard Manley Hopkins, not as a contribution to literary studies (for this I have not the competence), but as an acknowledgment of the debt I owe to that amazing poet for his contributions to theological reflection.

That task, if ever I get around to it, will have to await another occasion. But let this footnote be my notation of gratitude to my colleague and friend Nathan A. Scott, Jr., who, through the years in conversation and writing, has confirmed my conviction that theological anthropology steadily and almost proudly starves its perception and thins out its categories by neglect of the human dialogue with the natural world as this dialogue is movingly alive in so very large a sector of literature, old and new. A single instance of the enrichment that might accrue to theological reflection is Professor Scott's most recent volume, *The Wild Prayer of Longing* (New Haven: Yale University Press, 1971), and particularly the section devoted to the work of the late Theodore Roethke.

16. The "sense" of the church has always been sympathetic to the "sense for the world" articulated in this chapter. The church has permitted her children to sing some things the church has not ventured

to make propositions out of; she has, in fact, created the songs the children sing. However muted may have been any consistent or strong theology for nature, the church has clearly affirmed that the Lord of the Creation and the Lord of Redemption are one Lord; she has intuited and sung and prayed beyond her doctrines. The grace she affirms in her doctrine is postulated as related to nature—even if this postulation, frightened perhaps by pagan absolutizations of nature, has squeaked into her life via liturgy, paratheological documents, and hymnody. In the Prudentius hymn *Corde Natus Ex Parentis* we are called upon to "Let Creation Praise Its Lord, Evermore and Evermore"; the legends of Christmas include into the circle of a freshly manifested but ancient grace of God the cattle, the donkeys, and the sheep; the robin, in one fable, has its breast of red because he stood long at a fire, beating it into flame to keep the Christ-child warm.

Just as at the Nativity of the Christ the whole creation is involved in the nascent redemption, so at the death of Jesus the sense of the church has projected a gracious "sense for the world" in the natural convulsions that attend the passion narratives in the Gospels, and in the many legends of the Glastonbury-thorn genre (see, for instance, the magnificent Northumbrian poem "The Dream of the Rood").

17. Richard Wilbur, "Advice to a Prophet." © 1959 by Richard Wilbur. Reprinted from his volume, *Advice to a Prophet and Other Poems* by permission of Harcourt Brace Jovanovich, Inc.

## 6. Christian Theology and the Environment

1. Cf. Paul Ramsey, *Fabricated Man* (New Haven: Yale University Press, 1971).

2. Cf. Clifford Grobstein, *Strategy of Life* (San Francisco: W. H. Freeman, 1965).

3. Illustrative here is the work of Sir Herbert Dingle of the British Academy of Science, as reported in the *British Journal for the Philosophy of Science* 2 (1951): 86 ff., ". . . the Victorians looked upon the progress of science as a process of accumulation. . . . Our view today is different . . . the picture of the whole which we form in our attempt to express its interrelations undergoes unceasing transformations. . . . We can no longer say, the world is like this, or the world is like that. We can only say, our experience up to the present is best represented by a world of this character; I do not know what model will best represent the world of tomorrow, but I do know that it will co-ordinate a greater range of experience than that of today."

The late Percy Bridgman, a Harvard Professor of the Philosophy of Science, affirmed that there is no necessary connection between the thoughts in our minds and the way things are! (See P. W. Bridgman,

"The Way Things Are," in *The Limits of Language*, ed. Walker Gibson [New York: Hill and Wang, 1962], pp. 38–49.

4. For a difficult but rewarding essay on this point see Karl Rahner, *Nature and Grace* (London and New York: Sheed and Ward, 1963).

5. These essays are a monograph about a neglected and presently urgent *aspect* of grace; they are by no means a comprehensive treatise. It is necessary to stress this limited intention in order that the realm of the *human* as the primary realm for ethical response to God's creation shall not be understood as of lesser pathos and importance. Richard Neuhaus's *In Defense of People: Ecology and the Seduction of Radicalism* (New York: Macmillan, 1971), is a powerful and passionate statement of this primary realm of Christian ethical obedience that literally screams in anguish for ". . . the manifestation of the children of God." Even Mr. Neuhaus's attack upon the ecological movement as "diversionary" from the humanly demanding task for the poor, the powerless, the unjustly trapped—even his insightful pages about the slick operations of corporate monsters who, having had a large role in the raping and pollution of the earth, are now cashing in on the profits to be made from ameliorating the effects of their depredations, and disguising this tactic by a rhetoric of engagement and concern that approaches linguistic ethical pornography—must be heard and honored as the truth.

I share the main thesis of the Neuhaus book. Its appearance indeed makes it unnecessary to say again what he has said so well. But Mr. Neuhaus knows very well that the human brutality he records is of a piece with the less dramatic and quieter fault to which attention is called in these essays: i.e., that all abuse is a distortion of right use, for persons as for all things. What is not regarded as a grace will be disgraced into use without care.

This is the proper place to take notice of and record gratitude for Paul Santmire's *Brother Earth* (New York: Thomas Nelson, 1970). Summoning to his argument theological resources other than those I have called upon but equally well warranted in tradition and Christian confession, Mr. Santmire, too, has aimed at a renovation of Christian theology at its neglected center.

6. Theodore Roethke, "The Waking," *Words for the Wind* (Bloomington, Ind.: Indiana University Press, 1971), p. 114.

7. Professor Carl Braaten's *Christ and Counter-Christ* (Philadelphia: Fortress Press, 1971), while not focused upon the doctrine of grace, so elaborately details the theological and practical vitalities resident in the recovery of apocalyptic as central to Israel's faith, as the setting and transformed presupposition of the event of Jesus, and the promise, vision, and thrust toward liberation in history, that what

is said here about "vision" is given in that volume a very extended
and variously illustrated treatment.

8. The extensive literature produced by logicians, linguistic analysts,
and others, in search for a principle of verification of statements, suggests that the term "verification" may be too precise and too strong.
I think the term is open to the charge. But the deepening complexifi-
cation of the meaning of "verification" itself as the debate has moved
into a more accurate specification of the ambience of words and
sentences, the indeterminate intentionality of statements, the cultural
"career" of statements that transcend ostensive reference in virtue of
horizons "of possibility," etc.—this entire discussion seems to me to
give leave to ordinary reflection to reclaim the idea of verification
now that the "angels" who fear not to tread in that recondite region
are stomping one another in multiplication of qualifications.

9. This illustration is an extension of the truth and meaning of the
doctrine of justification into the area of material things; it is by no
means a transposition of the ground and origination of that doctrine
in the freedom and will of God whereby men are justified by nothing
other than the grace of God.